CARNIVORE 1 COOKBOOK FOR BEGINNERS

2000 Days of Carnivore Meals: A 101-Day Plan for Weight Loss, Energy Boost, and Mental Clarity with Simple, Delicious Recipes

Rowan Clarke

Table of Contents

Introduction

Welcome to the Carnivore Diet, a dietary approach that truly "goes against the grain." As one of the most restrictive diets, it emphasizes consuming only animal-based foods, completely eliminating all plant-based options. While this may seem extreme, it has gained popularity among those seeking an unconventional path to better health and well-being.

Welcome to the World of the Carnivore Diet

The Carnivore Diet is precisely as it sounds: a diet that consists solely of animal products. Unlike other dietary trends that advocate a balanced intake of fruits, grains, vegetables, and lean meats, the Carnivore Diet focuses exclusively on meat, fish, eggs, and animal-derived fats. It completely eliminates all sources of carbohydrates, including sugar, fiber, and starch found in plant-based foods.

Consider the Carnivore Diet as an ultra-restrictive version of the ketogenic or Paleo diets. While keto followers consume low-carb, high-fat foods, those on the Carnivore Diet take it a step further by excluding all plant foods, including vegetables, fruits, nuts, seeds, and even herbs. The diet centers exclusively on meat, fish, eggs, and animal fats, with water and salt being the only acceptable "extras."

The Carnivore Diet is not a new concept. Various cultures, from the Inuit of the Arctic to the Maasai of Africa, have thrived on high-fat, high-protein, animal-based diets for centuries. These communities demonstrate that humans can survive and even prosper on such a regimen. In recent years, advocates like Dr. Shawn Baker and Mikhaila Peterson have brought this diet into the mainstream by sharing their transformative health journeys.

The Science Behind the Carnivore Diet

To understand the Carnivore Diet, it's important to examine the science behind its potential benefits. Despite some controversy, it has garnered support from nutritional researchers and medical professionals who suggest it can be a potent tool for improving health markers, reducing inflammation, and enhancing metabolic health.

How Does the Carnivore Diet Work?

The Carnivore Diet shifts the body's primary energy source from carbohydrates to fats and proteins. In the absence of carbohydrates, the body enters ketosis, a state where fat is burned for energy instead of glucose. This metabolic shift can regulate blood sugar levels, reduce insulin spikes, and promote fat loss.

A significant feature of the Carnivore Diet is its effect on hormones. By cutting out carbohydrates, the diet lowers insulin production, which helps stabilize blood sugar levels and decrease hunger cravings. Moreover, animal proteins supply essential amino acids that promote muscle maintenance, support immune function, and contribute to overall health. The high fat content from animal products also enhances satiety, allowing individuals to feel full and satisfied with fewer meals.

Ketosis and the Carnivore Diet

Ketosis is a metabolic state where the body burns fat for energy instead of carbohydrates. The absence of carbs in the Carnivore Diet forces the body to rely on ketones, produced from fat breakdown, as its primary energy source. This shift not only promotes fat loss but also offers additional benefits, such as improved mental clarity, reduced inflammation, and more consistent energy levels.

Unlike the ketogenic diet, which permits low-carb vegetables, nuts, and some dairy, the Carnivore Diet completely excludes all plant-based foods, driving the body into a deeper state of ketosis. This sustained ketosis often results in more stable energy levels throughout the day, free from the typical spikes and crashes linked to carbohydrate intake.

The Role of Protein in the Carnivore Diet

Protein is a fundamental component of the Carnivore Diet. Animal-based proteins supply essential nutrients, such as B vitamins, iron, omega-3 fatty acids, and zinc, which are vital for muscle growth, tissue repair, hormone production, and immune function. This diet guarantees a complete amino acid profile, which can be challenging to obtain from plant-based sources.

Additionally, animal proteins are highly bioavailable, meaning the body absorbs and utilizes them more efficiently than plant-based proteins. This enhanced absorption supports muscle maintenance and growth, especially for those who engage in regular physical activity.

Health Benefits of the Carnivore Diet

While the Carnivore Diet is often criticized for its restrictive nature, many proponents claim a wide array of health benefits, ranging from weight loss to improved mental clarity. Let's explore some of the most commonly reported advantages.

- **Weight Loss and Body Composition:** A key advantage of the Carnivore Diet is its effectiveness for weight loss. The elimination of carbohydrates naturally reduces overall calorie intake due to the satiating effects of protein and fats, allowing individuals to consume fewer calories without consciously restricting their intake.

  Moreover, the Carnivore Diet's high-protein content enhances metabolism by increasing the thermic effect of food (TEF), which is the energy needed to digest, absorb, and metabolize nutrients. Since protein has a higher TEF than fats and carbohydrates, it requires more energy for processing, potentially supporting weight loss.

- **Reduced Inflammation:** Many individuals experience a notable reduction in inflammation-related symptoms on the Carnivore Diet. This may be attributed to the elimination of common inflammatory triggers found in plant foods, such as lectins, oxalates, and phytates. By focusing exclusively on animal-based foods, the diet helps reduce joint pain, improve skin conditions, and alleviate symptoms of autoimmune disorders in some cases.

- **Improved Mental Clarity and Mood:** Anecdotal evidence indicates that the Carnivore Diet enhances mental clarity, focus, and mood. This improvement may result from stabilized blood sugar levels and the absence of insulin spikes, which often impact cognitive function. Moreover, the diet's high-fat content supports brain health, given that the brain primarily consists of fat and depends on healthy fats for optimal functioning.

- **Enhanced Digestive Health:** Despite the common belief that fiber is essential for digestive health, many followers of the Carnivore Diet report improved digestion, reduced bloating, and less gastrointestinal discomfort. By removing plant fibers and other potential gut irritants, the diet may foster a healthier gut environment, alleviating symptoms of irritable bowel syndrome (IBS) and other digestive disorders.

- **Simplified Eating and Reduced Cravings:** The Carnivore Diet simplifies eating by eliminating the complexities of meal planning and calorie counting. With a focus on a limited number of food groups, making dietary choices becomes straightforward, without the need to worry about macronutrient ratios, portion sizes, or nutritional labels. Many followers also report a significant reduction in cravings, particularly for sugar and processed foods, making it easier to adhere to the diet over time.

Who Can Benefit from This Diet?

The Carnivore Diet might not be suitable for everyone, but it can be particularly beneficial for certain groups, especially those facing metabolic issues, autoimmune conditions, or food sensitivities.

1. **Individuals with Autoimmune Diseases**: Many autoimmune disorders, such as rheumatoid arthritis, lupus, and psoriasis, are often linked to chronic inflammation. As the Carnivore Diet is inherently anti-inflammatory, it may help reduce symptoms and enhance the quality of life for individuals with autoimmune conditions. By eliminating potential dietary triggers, this diet can assist in calming the immune system and promoting overall health.

2. **People Struggling with Weight Loss**: For those who have tried multiple diets without achieving lasting results, the Carnivore Diet offers a straightforward, effective approach to weight management. Its satiating nature, combined with the absence of carbohydrate-induced hunger, helps reduce overall calorie intake, allowing for weight loss without the sensation of deprivation.

3. **Individuals with Digestive Issues**: People suffering from digestive disorders like irritable bowel syndrome (IBS), Crohn's disease, or other gastrointestinal conditions may experience relief with the Carnivore Diet. The elimination of plant fibers and potential gut irritants allows the digestive system to rest and heal, often resulting in decreased bloating, gas, and discomfort.

4. **People with Mental Health Challenges**: Emerging evidence suggests that diet plays a significant role in mental health. The Carnivore Diet's emphasis on stable blood sugar levels, healthy fats, and essential nutrients can help improve mood, reduce anxiety, and support mental well-being. While more research is required, early indications show promise for individuals seeking to manage mental health through dietary interventions.

5. **Athletes and Active Individuals**: The high protein intake inherent to the Carnivore Diet supports muscle growth, recovery, and overall physical performance. This makes it an excellent option for athletes and those engaging in regular exercise. By focusing on nutrient-dense animal products, the diet provides all the amino acids necessary for muscle repair and growth, contributing to enhanced endurance and athletic performance.

Understanding the
Carnivore Diet

The Carnivore Diet has emerged as one of the most talked-about dietary trends in recent years, challenging traditional nutritional beliefs and offering a radical approach that focuses entirely on consuming animal-based foods.

What is the Carnivore Diet?

The Carnivore Diet is an extremely restrictive eating regimen that consists exclusively of animal-based foods. This means consuming only meat, fish, eggs, and animal-derived fats while completely excluding plant-based foods, including vegetables, fruits, grains, legumes, nuts, seeds, and even herbs and spices. It's a diet that prioritizes proteins and fats, minimizing or entirely eliminating carbohydrates.

Key Principles of the Carnivore Diet

- **Animal-Based Focus**: The diet emphasizes the consumption of whole animal products such as beef, pork, chicken, lamb, and fish. Other commonly included foods are eggs, bone marrow, organ meats (like liver and heart), and animal fats like butter and tallow.

- **Zero Carbohydrates**: One of the defining features of the Carnivore Diet is the complete absence of carbohydrates. The diet consists solely of fats and proteins, leading the body to enter a state of ketosis, where it burns fat as its primary energy source instead of glucose.

- **Simple and Unprocessed**: The Carnivore Diet encourages the consumption of unprocessed, whole foods. Followers are advised to avoid packaged and processed meats that contain added sugars, preservatives, or artificial ingredients.

- **Elimination of Plant Toxins**: A significant rationale behind the Carnivore Diet is the belief that many plant foods contain compounds like lectins, oxalates, and phytates, which can irritate the gut, trigger inflammation, and disrupt nutrient absorption. By eliminating plant foods, this diet aims to remove these potential irritants.

- **Hydration and Electrolytes**: Water, salt, and other electrolytes are crucial for maintaining hydration and proper bodily functions on the Carnivore Diet. Since plant-based sources of electrolytes like potassium and magnesium are excluded, followers must carefully manage their intake through diet and supplements.

History and Origins of the Carnivorous Diet

The Carnivore Diet may seem like a modern trend, but its origins date back thousands of years. Throughout history, various cultures and indigenous populations have thrived on animal-based diets, especially in environments where plant foods were either scarce or only available seasonally.

Ancestral Diets and Evolutionary Roots

Our early ancestors were primarily hunter-gatherers who relied on meat, fish, and animal fats as their main sources of nutrition. Before the development of agriculture, human diets were predominantly carnivorous, particularly in colder climates with limited plant food availability. Archaeological evidence indicates that early humans were skilled hunters who consumed large quantities of meat from megafauna like mammoths and other large herbivores. This nutrient-dense, animal-based diet is believed to have been crucial in the development of the human brain and the evolution of our species.

Indigenous Diets Around the World

Several indigenous groups, such as the Inuit of the Arctic, the Maasai of East Africa, and the Native American tribes of the Great Plains, have historically thrived on diets rich in animal products. For instance, the Inuit traditionally consumed a diet comprising seal, whale, fish, and caribou, with little to no plant foods. Similarly, the Maasai's diet was rich in meat, milk, and blood, demonstrating that humans can thrive on an animal-centric diet without experiencing significant nutritional deficiencies.

Modern Revival and Popularization

The contemporary Carnivore Diet has gained popularity thanks to advocates like Dr. Shawn Baker, a former orthopedic surgeon, and Mikhaila Peterson, who have openly shared their health transformations on this diet. These individuals have used their platforms to showcase the potential benefits of a meat-only diet, such as weight loss, improved mental health, and relief from autoimmune symptoms. Their experiences, along with growing anecdotal evidence, have sparked renewed interest in carnivorous eating, resulting in a rapidly expanding community of followers worldwide.

Fundamentals of Carnivore Nutrition

Understanding the nutritional composition of the Carnivore Diet is crucial for appreciating its potential benefits and limitations. This section will explore the primary nutrients obtained from animal-based foods and how they contribute to overall health.

Macronutrients: Protein and Fat

- **Protein**: Animal-based foods are excellent sources of high-quality protein, offering all nine essential amino acids necessary for muscle growth, tissue repair, hormone production, and immune function. The bioavailability of animal protein is higher than that of plant protein, meaning the body absorbs and utilizes it more efficiently.
- **Fat**: Fat serves as the primary energy source in the Carnivore Diet and is an essential component of this eating regimen. Healthy fats from animal products—such as saturated fats, monounsaturated fats, and omega-3 fatty acids—support cellular health, hormone production, and brain function. These fats also contribute to the diet's satiating effect, helping reduce hunger and food cravings.

Micronutrients: Vitamins and Minerals

- **Vitamins**: The Carnivore Diet provides an abundance of fat-soluble vitamins, including vitamins A, D, E, and K, which play vital roles in immune health, bone strength, vision, and cardiovascular function. Additionally, vitamin B12, found exclusively in animal products, is crucial for nerve function, DNA synthesis, and red blood cell formation.
- **Minerals**: Animal foods are rich in highly bioavailable minerals such as iron, zinc, selenium, and phosphorus, which are essential for oxygen transport, immune defense, enzymatic reactions, and bone health. However, it's important to monitor electrolytes like potassium and magnesium, which are typically obtained from plant sources, to ensure balanced intake

Absence of Antinutrients

One notable nutritional advantage of the Carnivore Diet is the absence of antinutrients commonly found in plants, such as lectins, oxalates, and phytates. These compounds can interfere with the absorption of essential nutrients and may cause digestive discomfort and inflammation in sensitive individuals.

Advantages and Disadvantages of the Carnivore Diet

While the Carnivore Diet has its supporters, it also presents potential drawbacks. This section provides a balanced overview of both the advantages and disadvantages.

Advantages of the Carnivore Diet

- **Simplified Eating**: The Carnivore Diet eliminates the complexities of meal planning and calorie counting. With only a limited selection of foods, it simplifies grocery shopping and meal preparation, making it easier to follow consistently.
- **Reduced Inflammation**: Many followers report a decrease in inflammation-related symptoms, such as joint pain, skin conditions, and autoimmune flare-ups. This benefit is often attributed to the elimination of plant toxins and antinutrients.
- **Enhanced Mental Clarity and Mood**: The stable blood sugar levels achieved through a zero-carb diet can lead to improved mental clarity, focus, and mood stability. Some individuals also report reduced anxiety and depressive symptoms, potentially due to the diet's positive effects on brain health.
- **Effective Weight Loss**: The high protein and fat content of the Carnivore Diet promotes satiety, leading to a natural reduction in calorie intake and weight loss without the need for strict portion control or restrictive eating.
- **Improved Digestive Health**: By removing fiber and plant-based irritants, many individuals experience relief from gastrointestinal issues, such as bloating, gas, and irritable bowel syndrome (IBS).

Disadvantages of the Carnivore Diet

- **Nutritional Deficiencies**: Although animal foods are nutrient-dense, excluding plant foods can lead to deficiencies in certain vitamins and minerals, such as vitamin C, potassium, and magnesium. Supplementation may be necessary for those who adhere to the diet long-term.
- **Potential Heart Health Concerns**: The high intake of saturated fats and cholesterol has raised concerns about potential effects on cardiovascular health. However, current research remains inconclusive, and individual responses to the diet may vary.
- **Social and Lifestyle Challenges**: The restrictive nature of the Carnivore Diet can make it difficult to participate in social events, dine out, or share meals with others, which may lead to feelings of isolation or challenges in maintaining the diet over time.
- **Lack of Long-Term Research**: While anecdotal evidence and short-term studies suggest potential benefits, there is a lack of long-term research on the health impacts of the Carnivore Diet. More studies are needed to fully understand its effects on overall health and longevity.
- **Adjustment Period and Potential Side Effects**: Many individuals experience an initial adjustment period when transitioning to the Carnivore Diet, often referred to as the "keto flu." Symptoms such as fatigue, headaches, and digestive changes may occur as the body adapts to a zero-carb regimen.

Getting Started with the Carnivore Diet

Transitioning to the Carnivore Diet can seem daunting, especially given its restrictive nature and the significant dietary changes it requires. However, with proper preparation, knowledge, and the right mindset, you can make the transition smoother and set yourself up for success.

Preparing for Transition: Tips and Tricks

Starting the Carnivore Diet involves more than simply changing what you eat—it requires a shift in mindset, daily habits, and nutritional understanding. Here are some tips and tricks to help ease your transition into this new way of eating.

Gradual Transition vs. Cold Turkey

There are two main approaches to starting the Carnivore Diet: jumping in all at once (cold turkey) or transitioning gradually by slowly eliminating plant-based foods from your diet.

- **Cold Turkey Approach**: This method involves immediately switching to an all-animal-based diet. It's suitable for those who are highly motivated and ready to make a complete change but may come with a more intense adjustment period, often referred to as the "keto flu," which includes symptoms like fatigue, headaches, and digestive changes.

- **Gradual Transition**: For those who prefer a slower approach, gradually removing plant foods over several weeks can help your body adjust more comfortably. Start by cutting out grains, sugars, and processed foods, then progressively eliminate vegetables, fruits, and dairy until you're fully carnivorous.

Stay Hydrated and Manage Electrolytes

The Carnivore Diet's lack of carbohydrates often leads to rapid water loss and a reduction in electrolyte levels, which can contribute to fatigue, muscle cramps, and dizziness. Proper hydration and electrolyte management are crucial for a smooth transition.

- **Drink Plenty of Water**: Aim to drink at least 8–10 glasses of water daily to stay hydrated, adjusting based on your activity level and climate.

- **Salt Your Food Generously**: Sodium is an essential electrolyte that helps maintain fluid balance and prevent dehydration. Adding extra salt to your meals can help replenish sodium lost during the initial phase of the diet.

- **Supplement If Needed**: Magnesium and potassium, commonly found in plant foods, may need to be supplemented on the Carnivore Diet. Magnesium supplements, in particular, can help prevent muscle cramps and improve sleep quality.

Embrace Simplicity in Meals

One of the appeals of the Carnivore Diet is its simplicity. Focus on easy-to-prepare meals that consist of basic animal-based ingredients. Cooking can be as straightforward as grilling a steak, scrambling eggs, or roasting a piece of chicken.

- **Batch Cooking and Meal Prep**: Preparing large quantities of meat in advance can save time and reduce the temptation to stray from the diet. Consider cooking multiple steaks, burgers, or chicken breasts and storing them in the fridge for quick access throughout the week.
- **Experiment with Different Cuts**: Variety is important to prevent food boredom. Explore different cuts of meat, such as ribeye, sirloin, pork chops, lamb shanks, and seafood, to keep your meals interesting and nutritionally balanced.

Listen to Your Body's Hunger Signals

The Carnivore Diet encourages you to eat when hungry and stop when full, without the need for calorie counting. Trust your body's natural hunger signals to guide your eating patterns. Some people may thrive on two larger meals per day, while others prefer three or more smaller meals.

- **Eat Until Satisfied**: Don't be afraid to eat larger portions, especially during the initial transition phase. It's normal for your appetite to increase as your body adapts to the higher fat and protein intake.
- **Don't Restrict Fat**: Fat is essential on the Carnivore Diet as it provides energy and helps keep you satiated. Be sure to include fatty cuts of meat, butter, and other animal fats in your meals.

Expect an Adaptation Period

As with any major dietary change, your body will need time to adjust to the Carnivore Diet. Common side effects during the first few weeks include changes in bowel movements, reduced energy, and cravings for carbohydrates. These symptoms are typically temporary and often referred to as the adaptation or "keto flu" phase.

- **Stay Committed**: Understanding that these symptoms are part of the adaptation process can help you stay committed. They usually resolve within a few weeks as your body becomes more efficient at burning fat for fuel.
- **Focus on Your Why**: Remind yourself why you chose the Carnivore Diet, whether it's for health improvement, weight loss, or other personal goals. Keeping your motivation front and center will help you persevere through the initial challenges

What to Eat: List of Allowed Foods

The Carnivore Diet is straightforward in its food choices but offers a variety of nutrient-dense options to keep you satisfied and nourished. Below is a comprehensive list of foods allowed on the Carnivore Diet:

Meats

- **Beef:** Ground beef, steak (ribeye, sirloin, filet), roast, brisket, ribs
- **Pork:** Pork chops, bacon (check for added sugars), pork ribs, sausage (without fillers)
- **Lamb:** Lamb chops, ground lamb, lamb shank, rack of lamb
- **Chicken:** Chicken thighs, drumsticks, wings, whole chicken, chicken liver
- **Turkey:** Turkey breast, ground turkey, turkey thighs

Fish and Seafood

- **Fish:** Salmon, sardines, mackerel, tuna, cod, halibut
- **Shellfish:** Shrimp, lobster, crab, clams, mussels
- **Oily Fish:** Rich in omega-3 fatty acids, these are excellent for heart and brain health.

Organ Meats

- **Liver:** Beef liver, chicken liver, lamb liver (nutrient-dense and rich in vitamins)
- **Heart:** Beef heart, chicken heart
- **Kidneys:** Beef kidneys, lamb kidneys

Eggs

- **Whole Eggs:** Chicken, duck, quail (rich in protein and healthy fats)
- **Egg Yolks:** A great source of fat-soluble vitamins and healthy cholesterol

Animal Fats

- **Butter:** Grass-fed if possible, for richer omega-3 content
- **Tallow:** Rendered beef fat, excellent for cooking
- **Lard:** Rendered pork fat, ideal for frying or sautéing
- **Duck Fat:** Flavorful and nutrient-rich, great for roasting vegetables if reintroducing some carbs later on.

Dairy (Optional and If Tolerated)

- **Cheese:** Hard cheeses, cream cheese (check for minimal additives)
- **Heavy Cream:** Low in carbohydrates, rich in fat
- **Full-Fat Yogurt:** Unsweetened, and ideally without additives

What to Avoid: Foods to Exclude

The Carnivore Diet strictly limits intake to animal-based products, meaning that many commonly consumed foods are off-limits. Here's a list of foods to avoid:

Plant-Based Foods

- **Vegetables:** All forms, including leafy greens, cruciferous veggies, and root vegetables
- **Fruits:** Including berries, apples, oranges, bananas, etc.
- **Grains:** Wheat, rice, oats, quinoa, and other grains
- **Legumes:** Beans, lentils, peas, chickpeas
- **Nuts and Seeds:** Almonds, peanuts, chia seeds, flaxseeds

Processed Foods

- **Sugars and Sweeteners:** Table sugar, honey, maple syrup, agave, artificial sweeteners
- **Packaged Snacks:** Chips, crackers, granola bars, protein bars
- **Processed Meats:** Sausages, hot dogs, and deli meats with added sugars or fillers
- **Oils and Fats**

    Plant Oils: Canola oil, sunflower oil, corn oil, soybean oil (high in omega-6 fatty acids and not recommended). In the strictest version of the Carnivore Diet, olive oil is generally not allowed since it is plant-based, and the diet focuses exclusively on animal products. The core principle of the Carnivore Diet is to consume only foods derived from animals, such as meat, fish, eggs, and animal fats like butter, tallow, and lard.

    However, some followers of a more flexible or modified version of the Carnivore Diet may choose to include small amounts of olive oil for cooking or flavor, especially if they are transitioning or not strictly adhering to the most rigid guidelines. For a fully Carnivore-compliant approach, we recommend replacing olive oil with butter, ghee, beef tallow, or lard, as these fats align more closely with the diet's animal-based principles

- **Margarine:** Artificially produced and often contains unhealthy trans fats

Beverages

- **Sugary Drinks:** Sodas, sweetened teas, sports drinks
- **Alcohol:** Especially those containing sugar or mixers; some opt to include occasional dry wine or spirits
- **Juices:** Fruit and vegetable juices, even if fresh-squeezed

Fitness Guide

Physical exercise is a powerful complement to any dietary approach, and the Carnivore Diet is no exception. While the diet provides a strong foundation for health and weight management, incorporating a fitness component can amplify its benefits, enhance overall well-being, and improve your body's ability to utilize nutrients efficiently.

The Benefits of Physical Exercise on the Carnivore Diet

Integrating physical exercise into your lifestyle while following the Carnivore Diet can offer numerous benefits for both physical and mental health. Here are some key advantages:

1. **Enhanced Fat Loss and Improved Body Composition**

Exercise, particularly resistance training and high-intensity interval training (HIIT), can accelerate fat loss and improve body composition by preserving lean muscle mass. The Carnivore Diet, being high in protein and healthy fats, naturally supports muscle maintenance and growth, making it an ideal partner to strength training.

- **Boost Metabolism:** Regular exercise increases your metabolic rate, helping you burn more calories even at rest. This can be especially beneficial on the Carnivore Diet, where your body is already primed to burn fat for fuel.
- **Maintain Muscle Mass:** Protein-rich diets like the Carnivore Diet provide essential amino acids needed for muscle repair and growth, which is crucial when engaging in strength training or resistance exercises.

2. **Improved Insulin Sensitivity and Blood Sugar Regulation**

Exercise enhances insulin sensitivity, helping your body better regulate blood sugar levels. On the Carnivore Diet, which is already low in carbohydrates, physical activity can further enhance these effects, potentially reducing the risk of type 2 diabetes and improving overall metabolic health.

- **Stabilize Blood Glucose Levels:** Strength training and aerobic exercises help your muscles utilize glucose more efficiently, stabilizing blood sugar levels and preventing spikes and crashes.
- **Reduce Insulin Resistance:** Regular exercise decreases insulin resistance, allowing your body to use glucose more effectively and reducing the need for insulin production.

3. **Enhanced Mental Clarity and Mood**

Exercise is widely recognized for its positive effects on mental health, including alleviating stress, anxiety, and depression—common issues during dietary changes. Physical activity boosts the release of endorphins, also known as "feel-good" hormones, which improve mood and mental clarity.

- **Boosts Endorphins:** Both cardio and strength training stimulate endorphin release, which can help alleviate low moods that some individuals experience when starting a new diet.
- **Improves Cognitive Function:** Physical activity enhances blood flow to the brain, improving cognitive function, focus, and overall mental sharpness, which are often positively impacted by the nutrient-rich profile of the Carnivore Diet.

4. **Increased Energy Levels and Reduced Fatigue**

The Carnivore Diet helps stabilize energy levels by providing consistent fuel from fats and proteins without the blood sugar fluctuations caused by carbohydrates. Incorporating exercise into your routine can further boost your energy, enhance stamina, and reduce overall feelings of fatigue.

- **Build Stamina:** Aerobic exercises such as walking, jogging, or swimming improve cardiovascular health, leading to greater endurance during daily activities and workouts.
- **Reduce Fatigue:** Regular physical activity helps combat tiredness, increases overall energy levels, and promotes better sleep quality, especially when paired with a diet high in nutrient-dense foods.

5. **Enhanced Cardiovascular Health**

While the Carnivore Diet emphasizes meat and animal products, cardiovascular exercise is essential for maintaining heart health. Activities like walking, cycling, and swimming can help improve heart rate, reduce blood pressure, and increase overall cardiovascular endurance.

- **Strengthen Heart Muscle:** Cardiovascular exercise strengthens the heart muscle, improving circulation and oxygen delivery to tissues throughout the body.
- **Lower Blood Pressure and Cholesterol:** Regular physical activity can lower blood pressure and improve cholesterol levels, even on a high-fat diet, contributing to better heart health.

6. **Supports Bone Health and Joint Function**

The high protein intake on the Carnivore Diet supports bone health by providing essential nutrients like phosphorus and calcium, which are vital for strong bones. Weight-bearing exercises further enhance bone density, making the combination of diet and exercise particularly beneficial for joint and bone health.

- **Increase Bone Density:** Resistance training and weight-bearing exercises help increase bone density, reducing the risk of osteoporosis and fractures.
- **Improve Joint Mobility:** Physical exercise keeps joints flexible and supports cartilage health, reducing the risk of stiffness and joint pain, which can be especially important for those with sedentary lifestyles.

Exercise Recommendations on the Carnivore Diet

When following the Carnivore Diet, certain types of exercise may complement your nutritional intake better than others. Here are some recommended workouts that align well with this dietary approach:

1. **Resistance Training (Strength Training)**

   Resistance training is highly effective on the Carnivore Diet, as the increased protein intake aids in muscle repair and growth. This type of exercise includes bodyweight exercises (such as push-ups and squats), weightlifting, and resistance band workouts.

   - **Build Muscle Mass**: Strength training stimulates muscle growth, helping you develop a toned and strong physique.
   - **Increase Metabolic Rate**: Building lean muscle boosts your resting metabolic rate, enabling your body to burn more calories even when you're not actively exercising.

2. **High-Intensity Interval Training (HIIT)**

HIIT workouts involve short bursts of intense activity followed by rest or low-intensity periods. This form of exercise is efficient and can provide cardiovascular benefits in a shorter time frame than traditional cardio.

   - **Boosts Fat Burning**: HIIT is excellent for fat burning, especially when paired with a diet that promotes fat utilization, like the Carnivore Diet.
   - **Time-Efficient**: HIIT workouts are often shorter but highly effective, making them ideal for those with limited time.

3. **Aerobic Exercise (Cardio)**

Aerobic exercises such as walking, jogging, swimming, and cycling are great for overall cardiovascular health. They help improve endurance, boost mood, and enhance cardiovascular function.

   - **Enhance Heart Health**: Regular cardio helps maintain a healthy heart and lungs, supporting overall fitness.
   - **Improve Endurance**: Consistent aerobic exercise builds stamina, making everyday activities easier and less tiring.

4. **Flexibility and Mobility Training**

Incorporating flexibility and mobility exercises, such as stretching, yoga, or Pilates, can improve joint function, reduce the risk of injury, and complement the muscle gains from strength training.

- **Improve Range of Motion**: Flexibility exercises help maintain joint flexibility, which is essential for an active lifestyle.
- **Reduce Injury Risk**: Stretching and mobility work can reduce muscle tightness and improve overall movement patterns, enhancing performance in other forms of exercise

Breakfast Recipes

1. Scrambled Eggs with Bacon

Difficulty level: ★☆☆☆☆
Preparation time: 5 minutes
Cooking time: 10 minutes
Servings: 2
Ingredients:

- 4 large eggs
- 4 strips of bacon
- 1 tbsp butter
- Salt, to taste

Directions:

1. Heat your skillet over medium heat then cook the bacon 'til crispy, about 5-7 minutes. Remove bacon then set aside, leaving the bacon fat in the skillet.
2. In your bowl, whisk the eggs with a pinch of salt.
3. Add butter to your skillet then melt it in a medium heat.
4. Place the eggs into your skillet and gently stir with a spatula 'til the eggs are softly scrambled, about 2-3 minutes.
5. Crumble cooked bacon then mix it into the scrambled eggs.
6. Serve hot.

Per serving: Calories: 290kcal; Fat: 24g; Carbs: 1g; Protein: 16g

2. Steak and Egg Skillet

Difficulty level: ★★☆☆☆
Preparation time: 5 minutes
Cooking time: 15 minutes
Servings: 2
Ingredients:

- 1 ribeye steak (about 8 oz)
- 4 large eggs
- 1 tbsp butter
- Salt and pepper, to taste

Directions:

1. Season steak using salt and pepper on both sides.

2. Heat your skillet over medium-high heat, add butter, then let it melt.
3. Sear the steak in the skillet for about 3-4 minutes per side for medium-rare, or 'til desired doneness. Remove steak from the skillet then let it rest.
4. In the same skillet, crack the eggs then cook to your preferred doneness, about 3 minutes for sunny-side-up.
5. Slice the steak and serve with eggs.

Per serving: Calories: 420kcal; Fat: 30g; Carbs: 0g; Protein: 38g

3. Beef Sausage Patties

Difficulty level: ★☆☆☆☆
Preparation time: 10 minutes
Cooking time: 10 minutes
Servings: 2
Ingredients:

- 8 oz ground beef
- 1 tsp salt
- ½ tsp black pepper
- ½ tsp garlic powder
- ½ tsp onion powder

Directions:

1. In your bowl, mix the ground beef with salt, pepper, garlic powder, and onion powder.
2. Form the mixture into 4 small patties.
3. Heat your skillet in a medium heat then cook the patties for about 4-5 minutes per side, 'til fully cooked.
4. Serve hot.

Per serving: Calories: 320kcal; Fat: 26g; Carbs: 1g; Protein: 21g

4. Pork Belly Breakfast Bites

Difficulty level: ★★☆☆☆
Preparation time: 5 minutes
Cooking time: 20 minutes
Servings: 2
Ingredients:

- 8 oz pork belly, cut into 1-inch cubes
- Salt, to taste

Directions:

1. Preheat your skillet over medium-high heat.
2. Add the pork belly cubes to your skillet then cook for 15-20 minutes, turning occasionally, 'til crispy and golden brown.
3. Season with salt and serve.

Per serving: Calories: 390kcal; Fat: 34g; Carbs: 0g; Protein: 17g

5. Ground Beef and Cheese Scramble

Difficulty level: ★☆☆☆☆
Preparation time: 5 minutes
Cooking time: 10 minutes
Servings: 2
Ingredients:

- 8 oz ground beef
- 4 large eggs
- ¼ cup shredded cheddar cheese
- 1 tbsp butter
- Salt, to taste

Directions:

1. Heat your skillet in a medium heat, add butter, then let it melt.
2. Add the ground beef then cook 'til browned, about 5-6 minutes. Season with salt.
3. In your bowl, whisk the eggs and pour them into your skillet. Stir gently to scramble the eggs with your beef.
4. Once the eggs are nearly set, sprinkle with shredded cheese and continue to cook 'til the cheese melts.

5. Serve hot.

Per serving: Calories: 360kcal; Fat: 28g; Carbs: 1g; Protein: 25g

6. Crispy Bacon and Fried Eggs

Difficulty level: ★☆☆☆☆
Preparation time: 5 minutes
Cooking time: 10 minutes
Servings: 2
Ingredients:

- 6 strips of bacon
- 4 large eggs
- Salt, to taste
- Black pepper, to taste

Directions:

1. Heat your skillet over medium heat and add the bacon strips. Cook 'til crispy, about 5-7 minutes. Remove bacon then set aside.
2. In the same skillet, crack the eggs and fry them in the bacon fat, seasoning with salt and pepper. Cook 'til the whites are set and the yolks are still runny, about 3-4 minutes.
3. Serve the fried eggs with crispy bacon on the side.

Per serving: Calories: 320kcal; Fat: 28g; Carbs: 1g; Protein: 17g

7. Ham and Cheese Omelet

Difficulty level: ★☆☆☆☆
Preparation time: 5 minutes
Cooking time: 5 minutes
Servings: 2
Ingredients:

- 4 large eggs
- 4 slices of ham, chopped
- ½ cup shredded cheddar cheese

- 1 tbsp butter
- Salt, to taste
- Black pepper, to taste

Directions:

1. Whisk the eggs in your bowl with a pinch of salt and pepper.
2. Heat your skillet over medium heat, add butter, then let it melt.
3. Pour the eggs into your skillet then let them set for about 1 minute.
4. Place the chopped ham and shredded cheese to one side of the omelet.
5. Fold the other side over then cook for another 1-2 minutes, 'til the cheese melts.
6. Serve hot.

Per serving: Calories: 340kcal; Fat: 27g; Carbs: 1g; Protein: 22g

8. Salmon and Cream Cheese Roll-Ups

Difficulty level: ★★☆☆☆
Preparation time: 10 minutes
Cooking time: None
Servings: 2
Ingredients:

- 4 slices of smoked salmon
- 4 tbsp cream cheese
- 1 tsp fresh dill, chopped (optional)

Directions:

1. Apply 1 tablespoon of cream cheese on each slice of smoked salmon.
2. Sprinkle with chopped dill, if using.
3. Roll up each slice tightly and slice into bite-sized pieces.
4. Serve immediately or chill for a few minutes.

Per serving: Calories: 250kcal; Fat: 21g; Carbs: 1g; Protein: 13g

9. Carnivore Breakfast Sausages

Difficulty level: ★☆☆☆☆
Preparation time: 10 minutes
Cooking time: 10 minutes
Servings: 2
Ingredients:

- 8 oz ground pork
- 1 tsp salt
- ½ tsp black pepper
- ½ tsp garlic powder
- ½ tsp onion powder

Directions:

1. Mix the ground pork with salt, pepper, garlic powder, and onion powder in your bowl.
2. Form the mixture into 4 small sausage patties.
3. Heat your skillet over medium heat then cook the patties for about 4-5 minutes per side, 'til fully cooked and browned.
4. Serve hot.

Per serving: Calories: 330kcal; Fat: 27g; Carbs: 1g; Protein: 18g

10. Egg and Beef Breakfast Bowl

Difficulty level: ★☆☆☆☆
Preparation time: 5 minutes
Cooking time: 10 minutes
Servings: 2
Ingredients:

- 8 oz ground beef
- 4 large eggs
- 1 tbsp butter
- Salt, to taste
- Black pepper, to taste

Directions:

1. Heat your skillet over medium heat, add butter, then let it melt.
2. Add ground beef then cook 'til browned, about 5-6 minutes. Season with salt and pepper.
3. In the same skillet, push the beef to one side and crack the eggs on the other side. Fry the eggs 'til the whites are set, about 3-4 minutes.
4. Serve the ground beef and eggs together in your bowl.

Per serving: Calories: 380kcal; Fat: 30g; Carbs: 1g; Protein: 23g

11. Pork Chops and Eggs

Difficulty level: ★★☆☆☆
Preparation time: 5 minutes
Cooking time: 15 minutes
Servings: 2
Ingredients:

- 2 pork chops (about 6 oz each)
- 4 large eggs
- 1 tbsp butter
- Salt, to taste
- Black pepper, to taste

Directions:

1. Season pork chops with salt and pepper.
2. Heat your skillet over medium-high heat, add butter, and sear the pork chops for about 5-7 minutes per side, 'til cooked through.
3. Remove pork chops then set aside.
4. In the same skillet, crack the eggs and fry to your desired doneness, about 3-4 minutes for sunny-side-up.
5. Serve the pork chops with the eggs on top.

Per serving: Calories: 400kcal; Fat: 32g; Carbs: 1g; Protein: 30g

12. Beef Liver and Egg Scramble

Difficulty level: ★★★☆☆
Preparation time: 5 minutes
Cooking time: 10 minutes
Servings: 2
Ingredients:

- 6 oz beef liver, thinly sliced
- 4 large eggs
- 1 tbsp butter
- Salt, to taste
- Black pepper, to taste

Directions:

1. Heat butter in your skillet over medium heat.
2. Add the beef liver slices then cook for about 3 minutes per side, 'til browned.
3. In your bowl, whisk the eggs with salt and pepper.
4. Pour the eggs into your skillet with the liver and scramble together 'til the eggs are cooked, about 2-3 minutes.
5. Serve hot.

Per serving: Calories: 300kcal; Fat: 20g; Carbs: 1g; Protein: 25g

13. Carnivore Pancakes

Difficulty level: ★☆☆☆☆
Preparation time: 5 minutes
Cooking time: 5 minutes
Servings: 2
Ingredients:

- 4 large eggs
- ½ cup crushed pork rinds
- 1 tbsp butter

Directions:

1. In your bowl, whisk the eggs then mix in the crushed pork rinds 'til a batter forms.
2. Heat your skillet over medium heat and add butter.

3. Pour the batter into your skillet, forming small pancakes. Cook for about 2-3 minutes per side 'til golden brown.
4. Serve immediately.

Per serving: Calories: 280kcal; Fat: 22g; Carbs: 1g; Protein: 18g

14. Cheese and Egg Muffins

Difficulty level: ★☆☆☆☆
Preparation time: 5 minutes
Cooking time: 15 minutes
Servings: 2
Ingredients:

- 4 large eggs
- ½ cup shredded cheddar cheese
- ¼ tsp salt
- ¼ tsp black pepper

Directions:
1. Preheat the oven to 375°F and grease a muffin tin.
2. In your bowl, whisk the eggs with salt and pepper, then stir in your shredded cheese.
3. Pour the mixture into 4 muffin cups, filling each halfway.
4. Bake for 12-15 minutes, 'til set and golden on top.
5. Serve warm.

Per serving: Calories: 220kcal; Fat: 18g; Carbs: 1g; Protein: 15g

15. Ribeye Steak and Eggs

Difficulty level: ★★☆☆☆
Preparation time: 5 minutes
Cooking time: 15 minutes
Servings: 2
Ingredients:

- 1 ribeye steak (about 10 oz)

- 4 large eggs
- 1 tbsp butter
- Salt, to taste
- Black pepper, to taste

Directions:

1. Season ribeye steak with salt and pepper on both sides.
2. Heat your skillet over medium-high heat, add butter, then let it melt.
3. Sear the steak for about 4-5 minutes per side, depending on your preferred doneness. Remove from skillet then let it rest.
4. In the same skillet, crack the eggs and fry them to your desired doneness, about 3-4 minutes for sunny-side-up.
5. Slice the steak and serve with the eggs on the side.

Per serving: Calories: 450kcal; Fat: 35g; Carbs: 0g; Protein: 34g

16. Chicken and Egg Scramble

Difficulty level: ★☆☆☆☆
Preparation time: 5 minutes
Cooking time: 10 minutes
Servings: 2
Ingredients:

- 6 oz chicken breast, diced
- 4 large eggs
- 1 tbsp butter
- Salt, to taste
- Black pepper, to taste

Directions:

1. Heat your skillet over medium heat, add butter, then let it melt.
2. Add the diced chicken breast then cook 'til browned then cooked through, about 5-6 minutes.
3. In your bowl, whisk the eggs with salt and pepper. Pour into your skillet with the chicken.
4. Stir gently to scramble eggs with the chicken 'til the eggs are fully cooked, about 2-3 minutes.
5. Serve hot.

Per serving: Calories: 280kcal; Fat: 18g; Carbs: 0g; Protein: 26g

17. Lamb Chop Breakfast Plate

Difficulty level: ★★☆☆☆
Preparation time: 5 minutes
Cooking time: 15 minutes
Servings: 2
Ingredients:

- 2 lamb chops (about 4 oz each)
- 4 large eggs
- 1 tbsp butter
- Salt, to taste
- Black pepper, to taste

Directions:

1. Season lamb chops with salt and pepper.
2. Heat your skillet over medium-high heat, add butter, and sear the lamb chops for about 4-5 minutes per side, 'til cooked to your liking. Remove then let rest.
3. In the same skillet, crack the eggs and fry 'til the whites are set, about 3-4 minutes.
4. Serve the lamb chops with the fried eggs on the side.

Per serving: Calories: 370kcal; Fat: 30g; Carbs: 0g; Protein: 24g

18. Meat and Egg Breakfast Burrito

Difficulty level: ★☆☆☆☆
Preparation time: 5 minutes
Cooking time: 10 minutes
Servings: 2
Ingredients:

- 6 oz ground beef
- 4 large eggs
- ¼ cup shredded cheese (optional)
- 1 tbsp butter
- Salt, to taste
- Black pepper, to taste

Directions:

1. Heat your skillet over medium heat, add butter, then let it melt.
2. Add the ground beef then cook 'til browned, about 5-6 minutes. Season with salt and pepper.
3. In your bowl, whisk the eggs and pour them into your skillet with the beef. Stir gently to scramble together.
4. If using cheese, sprinkle it over the mixture and continue to cook 'til the cheese is melted.
5. Serve as a hearty burrito-style scramble without a wrap.

Per serving: Calories: 320kcal; Fat: 26g; Carbs: 1g; Protein: 21g

19. Sausage and Cheese Frittata

Difficulty level: ★★☆☆☆
Preparation time: 5 minutes
Cooking time: 15 minutes
Servings: 2
Ingredients:

- 4 large eggs
- 4 oz sausage, crumbled
- ½ cup shredded cheddar cheese
- 1 tbsp butter
- Salt, to taste
- Black pepper, to taste

Directions:

1. Preheat the oven to 375°F.
2. Heat your skillet over medium heat, add the sausage, then cook 'til browned, about 5-6 minutes.
3. In your bowl, whisk the eggs with salt and pepper. Stir in your cooked sausage and shredded cheese.
4. Pour the mixture back into your skillet then cook for 2-3 minutes, just 'til the edges start to set.
5. Transfer your skillet to the oven then bake for 10 minutes, 'til the frittata is set and golden.
6. Serve warm.

Per serving: Calories: 350kcal; Fat: 28g; Carbs: 1g; Protein: 20g

20. Cheese-Stuffed Egg Bites

Difficulty level: ★☆☆☆☆
Preparation time: 5 minutes
Cooking time: 10 minutes
Servings: 2
Ingredients:

- 4 large eggs
- ¼ cup shredded mozzarella cheese
- 1 tbsp butter
- Salt, to taste
- Black pepper, to taste

Directions:

1. In your bowl, whisk the eggs with salt and pepper.
2. Heat a nonstick skillet over medium heat and add butter.
3. Pour half of the egg mixture into your skillet and sprinkle with cheese. Place the remaining egg mixture over the cheese.
4. Cook for about 4-5 minutes, flipping halfway, 'til the egg bites are fully set and the cheese is melted.
5. Slice and serve immediately.

Per serving: Calories: 220kcal; Fat: 18g; Carbs: 1g; Protein: 14g

Lunch Recipes

21. Grilled Chicken Breast with Butter

Difficulty level: ★☆☆☆☆
Preparation time: 5 minutes
Cooking time: 15 minutes
Servings: 2
Ingredients:

- 2 chicken breasts (about 6 oz each)
- 2 tbsp butter
- Salt, to taste
- Black pepper, to taste

Directions:

1. Preheat a grill pan over medium-high heat.
2. Season the chicken breasts using salt and pepper on both sides.
3. Bring the chicken on the grill then cook for 6-7 minutes per side, 'til fully cooked.
4. Melt butter in a mini pan or microwave.
5. Once the chicken is done, drizzle with melted butter and serve hot.

Per serving: Calories: 250kcal; Fat: 18g; Carbs: 0g; Protein: 24g

22. Crispy Pork Rind Crusted Chicken

Difficulty level: ★★☆☆☆
Preparation time: 10 minutes
Cooking time: 15 minutes
Servings: 2
Ingredients:

- 2 chicken thighs (about 6 oz each)
- ½ cup crushed pork rinds
- 1 egg, beaten
- 1 tbsp butter
- Salt, to taste

Directions:

1. Preheat the oven to 375°F.
2. Dip chicken thighs into the beaten egg, then coat them with crushed pork rinds.

3. Place the chicken on your baking sheet and drizzle with melted butter.
4. Bake for 15 minutes or 'til the chicken is crispy then cooked through.
5. Serve immediately.

Per serving: Calories: 350kcal; Fat: 26g; Carbs: 0g; Protein: 28g

23. Pan-Seared Ribeye with Garlic Butter

Difficulty level: ★★☆☆☆
Preparation time: 5 minutes
Cooking time: 15 minutes
Servings: 2
Ingredients:

- 1 ribeye steak (about 10 oz)
- 2 tbsp butter
- 2 garlic cloves, minced
- Salt, to taste
- Black pepper, to taste

Directions:

1. Season ribeye steak with salt and pepper on both sides.
2. Heat your skillet over medium-high heat, add 1 tbsp butter, then sear the steak for 4-5 minutes per side for medium-rare.
3. In the last minute of cooking, add the remaining butter and minced garlic to your skillet, basting the steak with the melted garlic butter.
4. Remove the steak then let it rest for a few minutes before slicing.
5. Serve with the garlic butter drizzled on top.

Per serving: Calories: 400kcal; Fat: 35g; Carbs: 0g; Protein: 28g

24. Beef Burger Patties with Cheese

Difficulty level: ★☆☆☆☆
Preparation time: 5 minutes
Cooking time: 10 minutes
Servings: 2
Ingredients:

- 8 oz ground beef
- 2 slices cheddar cheese
- 1 tbsp butter
- Salt, to taste
- Black pepper, to taste

Directions:

1. Form the ground beef into two patties and season with salt and pepper.
2. Heat your skillet over medium-high heat, add butter, then cook the patties for 4-5 minutes per side, 'til browned then cooked through.
3. Top each patty with a slice of your cheddar cheese then cook for an additional 1 minute 'til melted.
4. Serve hot.

Per serving: Calories: 300kcal; Fat: 25g; Carbs: 0g; Protein: 20g

25. Quick Grilled Lamb Chops

Difficulty level: ★★☆☆☆
Preparation time: 5 minutes
Cooking time: 10 minutes
Servings: 2
Ingredients:

- 4 lamb chops (about 4 oz each)
- 2 tbsp olive oil
- Salt, to taste
- Black pepper, to taste
- 1 tsp dried rosemary (optional)

Directions:

1. Preheat the grill to medium-high heat.

2. Rub the lamb chops using olive oil, salt, pepper, and rosemary, if using.
3. Place the lamb chops on the grill then cook for 4-5 minutes per side for medium-rare, or longer to your desired doneness.
4. Remove from the grill then let rest for a couple of minutes before serving.

Per serving: Calories: 350kcal; Fat: 28g; Carbs: 0g; Protein: 24g

26. Salmon Filets with Lemon Butter

Difficulty level: ★★☆☆☆
Preparation time: 5 minutes
Cooking time: 10 minutes
Servings: 2
Ingredients:

- 2 salmon filets (about 6 oz each)
- 2 tbsp butter
- 1 tsp lemon juice
- Salt, to taste
- Black pepper, to taste

Directions:

1. Preheat your skillet in a medium heat and add 1 tbsp of butter.
2. Season salmon filets with salt and pepper.
3. Place the salmon filets skin-side down in the skillet then cook for 4-5 minutes.
4. Flip the filets, place the remaining butter and lemon juice, then cook for another 3-4 minutes or 'til the salmon flakes easily.
5. Serve immediately with the lemon butter drizzled on top.

Per serving: Calories: 320kcal; Fat: 24g; Carbs: 0g; Protein: 26g

27. Pork Loin Cutlets

Difficulty level: ★★☆☆☆
Preparation time: 5 minutes
Cooking time: 10 minutes
Servings: 2
Ingredients:

- 4 pork loin cutlets (about 4 oz each)
- 1 tbsp butter
- Salt, to taste
- Black pepper, to taste

Directions:

1. Season pork cutlets with salt and pepper on both sides.
2. Heat your skillet in a medium-high heat and add the butter.
3. Once melted, add the pork cutlets then cook for 3-4 minutes per side 'til golden brown then cooked through.
4. Let the cutlets rest for a minute before serving.

Per serving: Calories: 270kcal; Fat: 18g; Carbs: 0g; Protein: 24g

28. Chicken Thighs with Skin-On

Difficulty level: ★★☆☆☆
Preparation time: 5 minutes
Cooking time: 20 minutes
Servings: 2
Ingredients:

- 4 chicken thighs, skin-on (about 6 oz each)
- 1 tbsp butter
- Salt, to taste
- Black pepper, to taste

Directions:

1. Preheat oven up to 400°F.
2. Season chicken thighs using salt and pepper on both sides.
3. Heat your skillet in a medium-high heat, add butter, and place the chicken thighs skin-side down. Sear for 5-6 minutes 'til the skin is crispy.

4. Flip the chicken thighs and transfer the skillet to the oven. Roast for 12-15 minutes or 'til fully cooked.
5. Serve hot.

Per serving: Calories: 320kcal; Fat: 26g; Carbs: 0g; Protein: 22g

29. Carnivore Tuna Salad

Difficulty level: ★☆☆☆☆
Preparation time: 5 minutes
Cooking time: 0 minutes
Servings: 2
Ingredients:

- 8 oz fresh tuna steak, seared and diced
- 1 tbsp olive oil
- 1 tsp lemon juice
- Salt, to taste
- Black pepper, to taste

Directions:
1. Dice the seared tuna steak and place it in your bowl.
2. Drizzle with olive oil and lemon juice.
3. Season using salt and pepper, then toss to combine.
4. Serve immediately as a light, fresh salad.

Per serving: Calories: 220kcal; Fat: 14g; Carbs: 0g; Protein: 22g

30. Sliced Roast Beef with Mustard

Difficulty level: ★☆☆☆☆
Preparation time: 5 minutes
Cooking time: 10 minutes
Servings: 2
Ingredients:

- 8 oz roast beef, thinly sliced

- 2 tbsp mustard (Dijon or yellow)
- 1 tbsp butter
- Salt, to taste
- Black pepper, to taste

Directions:

1. Heat your skillet over medium heat and add butter.
2. Add the sliced roast beef to your skillet and heat for 2-3 minutes, stirring occasionally, 'til warmed through.
3. Season with salt and pepper, if needed.
4. Serve with mustard on the side or drizzled on top.

Per serving: Calories: 280kcal; Fat: 22g; Carbs: 1g; Protein: 18g

31. Shrimp Skewers with Herb Butter

Difficulty level: ★★☆☆☆
Preparation time: 5 minutes
Cooking time: 8 minutes
Servings: 2
Ingredients:

- 12 large shrimp, peeled and deveined
- 2 tbsp butter
- 1 tsp garlic powder
- 1 tsp dried parsley
- Salt, to taste
- Skewers

Directions:

1. Preheat the grill to medium heat.
2. Thread shrimp onto skewers then season with salt, garlic powder, and parsley.
3. Grill shrimp skewers 2-3 minutes per side 'til the shrimp turn pink and are cooked through.
4. Melt the butter in a small pan and drizzle over the cooked shrimp before serving.

Per serving: Calories: 220kcal; Fat: 16g; Carbs: 0g; Protein: 18g

32. Simple Grilled Pork Tenderloin

Difficulty level: ★★☆☆☆
Preparation time: 5 minutes
Cooking time: 15 minutes
Servings: 2
Ingredients:

- 1 pork tenderloin (about 12 oz)
- 2 tbsp olive oil
- Salt, to taste
- Black pepper, to taste

Directions:

1. Preheat the grill to medium-high heat.
2. Rub pork tenderloin with olive oil, salt, and pepper.
3. Place the tenderloin on the grill then cook for 6-8 minutes per side 'til the internal temperature reaches 145°F.
4. Let your tenderloin sit for 5 minutes before slicing and serving.

Per serving: Calories: 290kcal; Fat: 18g; Carbs: 0g; Protein: 30g

33. Meatballs in Bone Broth

Difficulty level: ★★☆☆☆
Preparation time: 10 minutes
Cooking time: 20 minutes
Servings: 2
Ingredients:

- 8 oz ground beef
- 1 egg, beaten
- 1 tsp salt
- 1 tsp garlic powder

- 2 cups bone broth
- 1 tbsp butter

Directions:

1. In your bowl, mix the ground beef, beaten egg, salt, and garlic powder. Form into small meatballs.
2. Heat your skillet in a medium heat, add butter, and brown the meatballs for 5-6 minutes.
3. Pour the bone broth into your skillet and bring to a simmer.
4. Cover then cook for 10-12 minutes 'til the meatballs are cooked through.
5. Serve hot in the broth.

Per serving: Calories: 250kcal; Fat: 18g; Carbs: 1g; Protein: 18g

34. Pan-Fried Tilapia with Butter

Difficulty level: ★☆☆☆☆
Preparation time: 5 minutes
Cooking time: 10 minutes
Servings: 2
Ingredients:

- 2 tilapia filets (about 5 oz each)
- 2 tbsp butter
- Salt, to taste
- Black pepper, to taste
- 1 tsp lemon juice (optional)

Directions:

1. Heat your skillet in a medium heat and add butter.
2. Season tilapia filets with salt and pepper.
3. Cook the filets in the skillet for 4-5 minutes per side 'til golden and fully cooked.
4. Drizzle with lemon juice, if using, before serving.

Per serving: Calories: 210kcal; Fat: 16g; Carbs: 0g; Protein: 18g

35. Beef Ribs with Simple Seasoning

Difficulty level: ★★☆☆☆
Preparation time: 5 minutes
Cooking time: 2 hours
Servings: 2
Ingredients:

- 2 beef ribs (about 8 oz each)
- 2 tbsp olive oil
- 1 tsp salt
- 1 tsp black pepper

Directions:
1. Preheat the oven to 300°F.
2. Rub the beef ribs with olive oil, salt, and black pepper.
3. Place the ribs on your baking sheet lined with foil or parchment paper.
4. Bake for 2 hours or 'til tender.
5. Let rest for a few minutes before serving.

Per serving: Calories: 400kcal; Fat: 35g; Carbs: 0g; Protein: 24g

36. Grilled Flank Steak

Difficulty level: ★★★☆☆
Preparation time: 10 minutes
Cooking time: 8 minutes
Servings: 2
Ingredients:

- 1 flank steak (about 10 oz)
- 2 tbsp olive oil
- Salt, to taste
- Black pepper, to taste

Directions:

1. Preheat the grill to medium-high heat.
2. Rub the flank steak with olive oil, salt, and black pepper.
3. Grill the steak for 4 minutes per side for medium-rare, or longer for your desired doneness.
4. Remove from the grill then let rest for 5 minutes before slicing against the grain.
5. Serve immediately.

Per serving: Calories: 350kcal; Fat: 24g; Carbs: 0g; Protein: 32g

37. Carnivore Baked Meatloaf

Difficulty level: ★★☆☆☆
Preparation time: 10 minutes
Cooking time: 40 minutes
Servings: 2
Ingredients:

- 8 oz ground beef
- 1 egg
- 1 tsp salt
- 1 tsp black pepper
- 2 tbsp butter

Directions:
1. Preheat oven up to 375°F.
2. In your bowl, mix the ground beef, egg, salt, and black pepper 'til well combined.
3. Form the mixture into a loaf shape then place on your baking sheet.
4. Bake for 35-40 minutes, or 'til the meatloaf is cooked through.
5. Let rest for a few minutes before slicing.

Per serving: Calories: 300kcal; Fat: 24g; Carbs: 0g; Protein: 20g

38. Chicken Drumsticks with Ghee

Difficulty level: ★★★☆☆
Preparation time: 5 minutes
Cooking time: 35 minutes
Servings: 2
Ingredients:

- 4 chicken drumsticks (about 6 oz each)
- 2 tbsp ghee
- Salt, to taste
- Black pepper, to taste

Directions:

1. Preheat the oven to 400°F.
2. Rub the chicken drumsticks with ghee, salt, and black pepper.
3. Place the drumsticks on your baking sheet lined with parchment paper.
4. Bake for 30-35 minutes, or 'til the skin is crispy then the chicken is fully cooked.
5. Let rest for a few minutes before serving.

Per serving: Calories: 350kcal; Fat: 28g; Carbs: 0g; Protein: 24g

39. Bacon-Wrapped Chicken Breast

Difficulty level: ★★★☆☆
Preparation time: 10 minutes
Cooking time: 25 minutes
Servings: 2
Ingredients:

- 2 chicken breasts (about 6 oz each)
- 4 slices bacon
- Salt, to taste
- Black pepper, to taste

Directions:

1. Preheat the oven to 375°F.
2. Season chicken breasts with salt and pepper.

3. Wrap each chicken breast using 2 slices of bacon, securing with toothpicks if necessary.
4. Place on your baking sheet then bake for 20-25 minutes, or 'til the chicken is cooked through and the bacon is crispy.
5. Remove toothpicks and serve hot.

Per serving: Calories: 350kcal; Fat: 24g; Carbs: 0g; Protein: 30g

40. Beef and Cheese Roll-Ups

Difficulty level: ★☆☆☆☆
Preparation time: 5 minutes
Cooking time: 5 minutes
Servings: 2
Ingredients:

- 8 oz thinly sliced roast beef
- 2 oz cheese (e.g., cheddar, provolone)
- 1 tbsp Dijon mustard (optional)

Directions:

1. Lay out the roast beef slices and place a slice of cheese on top of each.
2. Roll up each beef slice with cheese inside.
3. Heat your skillet in a medium heat and add the roll-ups, cooking for 1-2 minutes per side 'til the cheese is melted and the beef is warmed through.
4. Serve immediately with mustard, if desired.

Per serving: Calories: 250kcal; Fat: 16g; Carbs: 0g; Protein: 22g

YOUR BONUSES

Scan the QR Code or visit the link below to access your 5 exclusive bonuses !

🎁 🎁 🎁 🎁 🎁

CLICK FOR BONUSES

Dinner Recipes

41. Ribeye Steak with Garlic Butter

Difficulty level: ★★★☆☆
Preparation time: 5 minutes
Cooking time: 15 minutes
Servings: 2
Ingredients:

- 2 ribeye steaks (about 8 oz each)
- 2 tbsp butter
- 2 cloves garlic, minced
- Salt, to taste
- Black pepper, to taste

Directions:
1. Preheat your skillet over medium-high heat.
2. Season the ribeye steaks with salt and black pepper.
3. Add the steaks to your skillet then cook 4-5 minutes per side for medium-rare, or to your preferred doneness.
4. In the last 2 minutes of cooking, add the butter and minced garlic to your skillet.
5. Spoon melted garlic butter over the steaks while they finish cooking.
6. Let the steaks rest for a few minutes before serving.

Per serving: Calories: 450kcal; Fat: 36g; Carbs: 1g; Protein: 30g

42. Baked Chicken Wings

Difficulty level: ★☆☆☆☆
Preparation time: 5 minutes
Cooking time: 40 minutes
Servings: 2
Ingredients:

- 10 chicken wings
- 2 tbsp olive oil
- Salt, to taste
- Black pepper, to taste

Directions:

1. Preheat oven up to 400°F.
2. Toss chicken wings with olive oil, salt, and black pepper.
3. Place the wings on your baking sheet lined with parchment paper.
4. Bake for 35-40 minutes, turning halfway through, 'til crispy then cooked through.
5. Serve hot.

Per serving: Calories: 320kcal; Fat: 22g; Carbs: 0g; Protein: 30g

43. Pork Tenderloin Medallions

Difficulty level: ★★☆☆☆
Preparation time: 5 minutes
Cooking time: 15 minutes
Servings: 2
Ingredients:

- 1 pork tenderloin (about 12 oz)
- 1 tbsp olive oil
- Salt, to taste
- Black pepper, to taste

Directions:
1. Preheat oven up to 375°F.
2. Slice pork tenderloin into medallions, about 1 inch thick.
3. Rub the medallions with olive oil, salt, and black pepper.
4. Heat your skillet in a medium-high heat and sear the medallions for 2-3 minutes per side.
5. Transfer the medallions to a baking sheet then bake for 8-10 minutes, or 'til cooked through.
6. Serve hot.

Per serving: Calories: 280kcal; Fat: 18g; Carbs: 0g; Protein: 28g

44. Seared Scallops with Butter

Difficulty level: ★★★☆☆
Preparation time: 5 minutes
Cooking time: 10 minutes
Servings: 2
Ingredients:

- 12 large scallops
- 2 tbsp butter
- Salt, to taste
- Black pepper, to taste

Directions:

1. Pat scallops dry using paper towels and season with salt and black pepper.
2. Heat your skillet in a medium-high heat and add butter.
3. Once butter is melted and hot, place the scallops.
4. Sear the scallops for 2-3 minutes per side 'til golden brown then cooked through.
5. Remove from the skillet and serve immediately.

Per serving: Calories: 250kcal; Fat: 18g; Carbs: 0g; Protein: 20g

45. Pan-Fried Cod Fillets

Difficulty level: ★☆☆☆☆
Preparation time: 5 minutes
Cooking time: 10 minutes
Servings: 2
Ingredients:

- 2 cod fillets (about 6 oz each)
- 2 tbsp olive oil
- Salt, to taste
- Black pepper, to taste

Directions:

1. Pat cod fillets dry using paper towels and season with salt and black pepper.
2. Heat olive oil (butter, if desired) in your skillet over medium heat.
3. Add the cod fillets then cook for 3-4 minutes per side, or 'til the fish is golden and flakes easily with a fork.
4. Serve hot.

Per serving: Calories: 250kcal; Fat: 16g; Carbs: 0g; Protein: 22g

46. Herb-Crusted Lamb Chops

Difficulty level: ★★★☆☆
Preparation time: 10 minutes
Cooking time: 15 minutes
Servings: 2
Ingredients:

- 4 lamb chops (about 6 oz each)
- 2 tbsp olive oil
- 1 tbsp dried rosemary
- 1 tbsp dried thyme
- Salt, to taste
- Black pepper, to taste

Directions:

1. Preheat the oven to 375°F.
2. Rub the lamb chops with olive oil (or butter, if preferred), rosemary, thyme, salt, and black pepper.
3. Heat an ovenproof skillet over medium-high heat then sear your lamb chops for 2-3 minutes per side.
4. Transfer skillet to the oven then bake for 10-12 minutes, or 'til the lamb is cooked to your desired doneness.
5. Let lamb chops rest for a few minutes before serving.

Per serving: Calories: 350kcal; Fat: 28g; Carbs: 0g; Protein: 22g

47. Grilled Sirloin Steak

Difficulty level: ★★★☆☆
Preparation time: 5 minutes
Cooking time: 10 minutes
Servings: 2
Ingredients:

- 2 sirloin steaks (about 8 oz each)
- 2 tbsp olive oil
- Salt, to taste
- Black pepper, to taste

Directions:

1. Preheat the grill to medium-high heat.
2. Rub the sirloin steaks with olive oil, salt, and black pepper.
3. Grill steaks 4-5 minutes per side for medium-rare, or to your desired doneness.
4. Let the steaks rest for a few minutes before serving.

Per serving: Calories: 350kcal; Fat: 22g; Carbs: 0g; Protein: 32g

48. Beef Kebabs with Simple Seasoning

Difficulty level: ★★★☆☆
Preparation time: 10 minutes
Cooking time: 10 minutes
Servings: 2
Ingredients:

- 12 oz beef sirloin, cut into cubes
- 2 tbsp olive oil
- 1 tsp salt
- 1 tsp black pepper
- 1 tsp paprika (optional)
- Skewers

Directions:

1. Preheat the grill to medium-high heat.
2. Toss the beef cubes with olive oil, salt, black pepper, and paprika if using.
3. Thread the beef cubes onto skewers.
4. Grill the kebabs for 3-4 minutes per side, or 'til the beef is cooked to your desired doneness.
5. Serve hot.

Per serving: Calories: 300kcal; Fat: 20g; Carbs: 0g; Protein: 26g

49. Pork Shoulder Steaks

Difficulty level: ★★★☆☆
Preparation time: 10 minutes
Cooking time: 20 minutes
Servings: 2
Ingredients:

- 2 pork shoulder steaks (about 8 oz each)
- 2 tbsp olive oil
- Salt, to taste
- Black pepper, to taste

Directions:

1. Preheat your skillet in a medium-high heat.
2. Rub the pork shoulder steaks with olive oil, salt, and black pepper.
3. Sear the steaks in the skillet for 5-7 minutes per side, or 'til browned then cooked through.
4. Let the steaks rest for a few minutes before serving.

Per serving: Calories: 350kcal; Fat: 28g; Carbs: 0g; Protein: 24g

50. Oven-Roasted Turkey Legs

Difficulty level: ★★★☆☆
Preparation time: 10 minutes
Cooking time: 1 hour
Servings: 2
Ingredients:

- 2 turkey legs (about 8 oz each)
- 2 tbsp olive oil
- Salt, to taste
- Black pepper, to taste
- 1 tsp dried thyme (optional)

Directions:

1. Preheat the oven to 375°F.
2. Rub the turkey legs with olive oil, salt, black pepper, and dried thyme if using.
3. Place the turkey legs on your baking sheet lined with parchment paper.
4. Roast for 55-60 minutes, or 'til the turkey is cooked through and the skin is crispy.

5. Let rest for a few minutes before serving.

Per serving: Calories: 400kcal; Fat: 28g; Carbs: 0g; Protein: 3

51. Butter-Basted Shrimp

Difficulty level: ★★★☆☆
Preparation time: 5 minutes
Cooking time: 10 minutes
Servings: 2
Ingredients:

- 12 large shrimp, peeled and deveined
- 2 tbsp butter
- Salt, to taste
- Black pepper, to taste
- 2 cloves garlic, minced (optional)

Directions:
1. Heat your skillet over medium heat then melt the butter.
2. Add the garlic if using and sauté for 1 minute 'til fragrant.
3. Add shrimp to your skillet then cook for 2-3 minutes per side, or 'til pink and opaque.
4. Season using salt and black pepper, then toss in the butter to coat.
5. Serve immediately.

Per serving: Calories: 280kcal; Fat: 20g; Carbs: 0g; Protein: 22g

52. Pan-Seared Salmon Steaks

Difficulty level: ★★★☆☆
Preparation time: 5 minutes
Cooking time: 10 minutes
Servings: 2
Ingredients:

- 2 salmon steaks (about 6 oz each)
- 2 tbsp olive oil
- Salt, to taste
- Black pepper, to taste

Directions:
1. Heat olive oil in your skillet over medium-high heat.

2. Season salmon steaks with salt and black pepper.
3. Add the salmon steaks to your skillet and sear for 4-5 minutes per side, or 'til cooked to your liking.
4. Serve hot.

Per serving: Calories: 320kcal; Fat: 22g; Carbs: 0g; Protein: 28g

53. Beef Tenderloin Tips

Difficulty level: ★★★☆☆
Preparation time: 10 minutes
Cooking time: 10 minutes
Servings: 2
Ingredients:

- 12 oz beef tenderloin, cut into bite-sized tips
- 2 tbsp olive oil
- Salt, to taste
- Black pepper, to taste
- 1 tsp garlic powder (optional)

Directions:

1. Heat olive oil in your skillet over medium-high heat.
2. Season the beef tenderloin tips with salt, black pepper, and garlic powder if using.
3. Add the beef tips to your skillet then cook for 2-3 minutes per side, or 'til browned then cooked to your desired doneness.
4. Serve hot.

Per serving: Calories: 320kcal; Fat: 20g; Carbs: 0g; Protein: 32g

54. Lamb Burgers with Cheese

Difficulty level: ★★★☆☆
Preparation time: 10 minutes
Cooking time: 10 minutes
Servings: 2
Ingredients:

- 8 oz ground lamb

- 2 slices cheddar cheese
- 1 tbsp olive oil
- Salt, to taste
- Black pepper, to taste

Directions:

1. Preheat your skillet over medium-high heat.
2. Form the ground lamb into 2 patties and season with salt and black pepper.
3. Cook the lamb patties in the skillet for 4-5 minutes per side, or 'til cooked through.
4. Place a slice of your cheddar cheese on each patty in the last minute of cooking, allowing it to melt.
5. Serve hot.

Per serving: Calories: 370kcal; Fat: 28g; Carbs: 0g; Protein: 26g

55. Pork Spare Ribs

Difficulty level: ★★★☆☆
Preparation time: 10 minutes
Cooking time: 1 hour
Servings: 2
Ingredients:

- 1 lb pork spare ribs
- 2 tbsp olive oil
- Salt, to taste
- Black pepper, to taste
- 1 tsp smoked paprika (optional)

Directions:

1. Preheat the oven to 375°F.
2. Rub the pork spare ribs with black pepper, olive oil, salt, and smoked paprika if using.
3. Place the ribs on your baking sheet lined with parchment paper.
4. Roast for 50-60 minutes, or 'til the ribs are tender then cooked through.
5. Let rest for a few minutes before cutting into portions.

Per serving: Calories: 400kcal; Fat: 30g; Carbs: 0g; Protein: 28g

56. Seared Ahi Tuna

Difficulty level: ★★★☆☆
Preparation time: 5 minutes
Cooking time: 5 minutes
Servings: 2
Ingredients:

- 2 ahi tuna steaks (about 6 oz each)
- 2 tbsp olive oil
- Salt, to taste
- Black pepper, to taste
- 1 tsp sesame seeds (optional)

Directions:

1. Heat olive oil in your skillet over medium-high heat.
2. Season tuna steaks with salt and black pepper.
3. Add the tuna steaks to your skillet and sear for 2-3 minutes per side, or 'til the outside is browned but the inside is rare.
4. Sprinkle with sesame seeds if desired.
5. Serve immediately.

Per serving: Calories: 250kcal; Fat: 16g; Carbs: 0g; Protein: 24g

57. Beef Strip Loin

Difficulty level: ★★★☆☆
Preparation time: 5 minutes
Cooking time: 15 minutes
Servings: 2
Ingredients:

- 2 beef strip loins (about 8 oz each)
- 2 tbsp olive oil
- Salt, to taste
- Black pepper, to taste

Directions:

1. Preheat your skillet over medium-high heat.

2. Rub the beef strip loins with olive oil, salt, and black pepper.
3. Add the strip loins to your skillet and sear for 5-7 minutes per side, or 'til cooked to your desired doneness.
4. Let the beef rest for a few minutes before serving.

Per serving: Calories: 350kcal; Fat: 22g; Carbs: 0g; Protein: 32g

58. Sautéed Chicken Hearts

Difficulty level: ★★★☆☆
Preparation time: 5 minutes
Cooking time: 10 minutes
Servings: 2
Ingredients:

- 8 oz chicken hearts
- 2 tbsp olive oil
- Salt, to taste
- Black pepper, to taste
- 1 tsp dried oregano (optional)

Directions:

1. Heat olive oil in your skillet in a medium heat.
2. Season the chicken hearts with salt, black pepper, and dried oregano if using.
3. Sauté the chicken hearts for 5-7 minutes, or 'til cooked through and slightly crispy.
4. Serve hot.

Per serving: Calories: 200kcal; Fat: 12g; Carbs: 0g; Protein: 24

59. Pork Ribeye Chops

Difficulty level: ★★★☆☆
Preparation time: 10 minutes
Cooking time: 15 minutes
Servings: 2
Ingredients:

- 2 pork ribeye chops (about 8 oz each)
- 2 tbsp olive oil
- Salt, to taste
- Black pepper, to taste

- 1 tsp paprika (optional)

Directions:

1. Preheat your skillet over medium-high heat.
2. Rub the pork ribeye chops with olive oil, salt, black pepper, and paprika if using.
3. Sear the chops in the skillet for 6-7 minutes per side, or 'til cooked through.
4. Serve hot.

Per serving: Calories: 350kcal; Fat: 26g; Carbs: 0g; Protein: 28g

60. Baked Meat and Cheese Casserole

Difficulty level: ★★★☆☆
Preparation time: 10 minutes
Cooking time: 30 minutes
Servings: 2
Ingredients:

- 1 lb ground beef
- 1 cup shredded cheddar cheese
- 1 cup heavy cream
- 1 egg
- Salt, to taste
- Black pepper, to taste

Directions:

1. Preheat the oven to 375°F.
2. Cook the ground beef in your skillet in a medium heat 'til browned, then drain excess fat.
3. In mixing bowl, combine cooked beef, heavy cream, egg, salt, and black pepper.
4. Bring the mixture to a baking dish then top with shredded cheddar cheese.
5. Bake for 25-30 minutes, or 'til the cheese is melted and bubbly.
6. Let cool for a few minutes before serving.

Per serving: Calories: 450kcal; Fat: 32g; Carbs: 3g; Protein: 36g

Snack Recipes

61. Beef Jerky

Difficulty level: ★★★☆☆
Preparation time: 15 minutes
Cooking time: 6-8 hours
Servings: 4
Ingredients:

- 1 lb beef sirloin, thinly sliced
- 1/4 cup soy sauce
- 1/4 cup Worcestershire sauce
- 2 tbsp olive oil
- 1 tsp black pepper
- 1 tsp garlic powder

Directions:

1. In your bowl, mix soy sauce, Worcestershire sauce, olive oil, black pepper, and garlic powder.
2. Marinate the beef slices in the mixture for at least 4 hours or overnight in the refrigerator.
3. Preheat oven up to 160°F.
4. Arrange the beef slices on a baking rack set over a baking sheet.
5. Bake for 6-8 hours, or 'til the jerky is dry and chewy.
6. Let cool before storing.

Per serving: Calories: 180kcal; Fat: 8g; Carbs: 2g; Protein: 24g

62. Crispy Chicken Skins

Difficulty level: ★☆☆☆☆
Preparation time: 5 minutes
Cooking time: 15 minutes
Servings: 2
Ingredients:

- 8 oz chicken skin, cut into pieces
- Salt, to taste
- Black pepper, to taste

Directions:

1. Preheat the oven to 375°F and line a baking sheet with parchment paper.

2. Arrange the chicken skin pieces in a one layer on your baking sheet.
3. Season with salt and black pepper.
4. Bake for 15-20 minutes, or 'til the skins are crispy.
5. Let cool before serving.

Per serving: Calories: 220kcal; Fat: 22g; Carbs: 0g; Protein: 10g

63. Bacon Chips

Difficulty level: ★☆☆☆☆
Preparation time: 5 minutes
Cooking time: 10 minutes
Servings: 2
Ingredients:

- 8 slices of bacon

Directions:
1. Preheat the oven to 400°F and line a baking sheet with parchment paper.
2. Arrange the bacon slices in a one layer on your baking sheet.
3. Bake for 10-12 minutes, or 'til crispy.
4. Remove the bacon from the oven then place on paper towels to drain excess fat.
5. Let cool before serving.

Per serving: Calories: 200kcal; Fat: 18g; Carbs: 0g; Protein: 12g

64. Ham Roll-Ups

Difficulty level: ★☆☆☆☆
Preparation time: 5 minutes
Cooking time: 0 minutes
Servings: 2
Ingredients:

- 8 slices of ham
- 4 oz cream cheese, softened
- 1 tbsp mustard (optional)

Directions:

1. Apply thin layer of your cream cheese on each slice of ham.
2. Roll up the ham slices tightly.
3. Slice each roll-up in half and serve.

Per serving: Calories: 180kcal; Fat: 14g; Carbs: 1g; Protein: 12g

65. Pork Rind Nachos

Difficulty level: ★☆☆☆☆
Preparation time: 5 minutes
Cooking time: 5 minutes
Servings: 2
Ingredients:

- 2 cups pork rinds
- 1/2 cup shredded cheddar cheese
- 1/4 cup sour cream
- 2 tbsp sliced jalapeños (optional)

Directions:

1. Preheat the oven to 375°F.
2. Arrange the pork rinds on your baking sheet.
3. Sprinkle your shredded cheddar cheese equally over the pork rinds.
4. Bake for 5 minutes, or 'til the cheese is melted.
5. Top with sour cream and sliced jalapeños if desired.

Per serving: Calories: 300kcal; Fat: 24g; Carbs: 2g; Protein: 15g

66. Smoked Salmon Slices

Difficulty level: ★☆☆☆☆
Preparation time: 5 minutes
Cooking time: 0 minutes
Servings: 2
Ingredients:

- 4 oz smoked salmon
- 1 tbsp capers (optional)
- 1 tbsp cream cheese (optional)

Directions:

1. Arrange the smoked salmon slices on a plate.
2. Top with capers and cream cheese if desired.
3. Serve immediately.

Per serving: Calories: 180kcal; Fat: 12g; Carbs: 0g; Protein: 18g

67. Meat Sticks

Difficulty level: ★★★☆☆
Preparation time: 20 minutes
Cooking time: 3-4 hours
Servings: 4
Ingredients:

- 1 lb ground beef
- 1/4 cup soy sauce
- 1 tsp black pepper
- 1 tsp garlic powder
- 1 tsp paprika

Directions:

1. Preheat the oven to 175°F.
2. In your bowl, combine ground beef, soy sauce, black pepper, garlic powder, and paprika.
3. Shape the mixture into thin sticks and place them on a baking rack set over your baking sheet.
4. Bake for 3-4 hours, or 'til the meat sticks are dry and firm.
5. Let cool before storing.

Per serving: Calories: 200kcal; Fat: 12g; Carbs: 2g; Protein: 22g

68. Pepperoni Slices

Difficulty level: ★☆☆☆☆
Preparation time: 5 minutes
Cooking time: 5 minutes
Servings: 2
Ingredients:

- 20 slices of pepperoni

Directions:

1. Preheatthe oven to 375°F and line a baking sheet with parchment paper.
2. Arrange the pepperoni slices in a one layer on your baking sheet.
3. Bake for 5 minutes, or 'til the edges are crispy.
4. Let cool before serving.

Per serving: Calories: 180kcal; Fat: 16g; Carbs: 0g; Protein: 8g

69. Sliced Beef Jerky Chips

Difficulty level: ★★★☆☆
Preparation time: 10 minutes
Cooking time: 6-8 hours
Servings: 4
Ingredients:

- 1 lb beef jerky, sliced into thin strips

Directions:

1. Preheat the oven to 160°F.
2. Arrange the beef jerky strips in a one layer on a baking rack set over a baking sheet.
3. Bake for 6-8 hours, or 'til the jerky is dry and crispy.
4. Let cool before serving.

Per serving: Calories: 200kcal; Fat: 12g; Carbs: 1g; Protein: 22g

70. Prosciutto-Wrapped Mozzarella

Difficulty level: ★☆☆☆☆
Preparation time: 5 minutes
Cooking time: 0 minutes
Servings: 2
Ingredients:

- 8 slices of prosciutto
- 4 oz mozzarella cheese, cut into 8 sticks

Directions:
1. Wrap each mozzarella stick with a slice of prosciutto.
2. Serve immediately or chill 'til ready to eat.

Per serving: Calories: 200kcal; Fat: 16g; Carbs: 1g; Protein: 14g

71. Mini Meatballs

Difficulty level: ★★★☆☆
Preparation time: 10 minutes
Cooking time: 15 minutes
Servings: 2
Ingredients:

- 1 lb ground beef
- 1 egg
- 1/4 cup grated Parmesan cheese
- 1 tsp dried oregano (optional)
- Salt, to taste
- Black pepper, to taste

Directions:
1. Preheat the oven to 375°F and line a baking sheet with parchment paper.
2. In your bowl, combine ground beef, egg, Parmesan cheese, oregano (if using), salt, and black pepper.
3. Form the mixture into small meatballs and place them on your baking sheet.
4. Bake for 15 minutes, or 'til cooked through.
5. Let cool slightly before serving.

Per serving: Calories: 250kcal; Fat: 18g; Carbs: 1g; Protein: 22g

72. Egg Salad

Difficulty level: ★★★☆☆
Preparation time: 15 minutes
Cooking time: 10 minutes
Servings: 2
Ingredients:

- 6 large eggs
- 2 tbsp mayonnaise
- 2 tbsp chopped fresh chives (optional)
- Salt, to taste
- Black pepper, to taste

Directions:
1. Boil eggs by placing them in your pot of cold water. Boil, then reduce heat then simmer for 10 minutes.
2. Bring the eggs to a bowl of ice water to cool. Peel and chop.
3. In a bowl, combine chopped eggs, mayonnaise, chives (if using), salt, and black pepper.
4. Mix until well combined.
5. Serve chilled.

Per serving: Calories: 250kcal; Fat: 20g; Carbs: 1g; Protein: 14g

73. Shrimp Cocktail

Difficulty level: ★☆☆☆☆
Preparation time: 10 minutes
Cooking time: 5 minutes
Servings: 2
Ingredients:

- 1 lb large shrimp, peeled and deveined
- 1 tbsp olive oil
- 1 tsp paprika
- Salt, to taste
- Black pepper, to taste

Directions:

1. Preheat your skillet over medium-high heat and add olive oil.
2. Season the shrimp with paprika, salt, and black pepper.
3. Sauté the shrimp in the skillet for 2-3 minutes per side, or 'til pink and opaque.
4. Remove from heat then let cool.
5. Serve chilled or at room temperature.

Per serving: Calories: 180kcal; Fat: 6g; Carbs: 0g; Protein: 30g

74. Chicken Sausage Bites

Difficulty level: ★☆☆☆☆
Preparation time: 5 minutes
Cooking time: 10 minutes
Servings: 2
Ingredients:

- 2 chicken sausages
- 1 tbsp olive oil

Directions:
1. Slice the chicken sausages into bite-sized pieces.
2. Heat olive oil in your skillet in a medium heat.
3. Add the sausage pieces then cook for 8-10 minutes, or 'til browned then cooked through.
4. Serve hot.

Per serving: Calories: 200kcal; Fat: 14g; Carbs: 0g; Protein: 18g

75. Pork Cracklings

Difficulty level: ★☆☆☆☆
Preparation time: 5 minutes
Cooking time: 15 minutes
Servings: 2
Ingredients:

- 2 cups pork rinds
- Salt, to taste

Directions:

1. Preheat oven up to 400°F.
2. Arrange the pork rinds in a one layer on your baking sheet.
3. Bake for 15 minutes, or 'til crispy.
4. Season with salt to taste.
5. Let cool before serving.

Per serving: Calories: 220kcal; Fat: 22g; Carbs: 0g; Protein: 10g

76. Carnivore Cheese Board

Difficulty level: ★☆☆☆☆
Preparation time: 10 minutes
Cooking time: 0 minutes
Servings: 2
Ingredients:

- 4 oz cheddar cheese, sliced
- 4 oz Gouda cheese, sliced
- 4 oz aged Parmesan, cubed
- 8 slices of pepperoni

Directions:

1. Arrange the cheese slices, cheese cubes, and pepperoni slices on a platter.
2. Serve immediately or chill 'til ready to eat.

Per serving: Calories: 400kcal; Fat: 32g; Carbs: 2g; Protein: 25g

77. Liver Pate Bites

Difficulty level: ★★★☆☆
Preparation time: 15 minutes
Cooking time: 10 minutes
Servings: 2
Ingredients:

- 1/2 lb chicken liver
- 1/4 cup unsalted butter

- 1 small onion, chopped
- 1 garlic clove, minced
- Salt, to taste
- Black pepper, to taste

Directions:
1. In a skillet, melt butter in a medium heat and sauté the onion and garlic 'til softened.
2. Add the chicken liver then cook 'til browned then cooked through, about 10 minutes.
3. Season with salt and black pepper.
4. Bring the mixture to your food processor and blend 'til smooth.
5. Chill before serving.

Per serving: Calories: 180kcal; Fat: 14g; Carbs: 2g; Protein: 12g

78. Sliced Salami

Difficulty level: ★☆☆☆☆
Preparation time: 5 minutes
Cooking time: 0 minutes
Servings: 2
Ingredients:

- 8 slices of salami

Directions:
1. Arrange the salami slices on a plate.
2. Serve immediately or chill 'til ready to eat.

Per serving: Calories: 150kcal; Fat: 12g; Carbs: 0g; Protein: 8g

79. Chicken Liver Mousse

Difficulty level: ★★★☆☆
Preparation time: 15 minutes
Cooking time: 15 minutes
Servings: 2
Ingredients:

- 1/2 lb chicken livers
- 1/4 cup unsalted butter

- 1/4 cup heavy cream
- 1 small onion, chopped
- 1 garlic clove, minced
- Salt, to taste
- Black pepper, to taste

Directions:

1. In a skillet, melt butter in a medium heat and sauté the onion and garlic 'til softened.
2. Add the chicken livers then cook 'til browned then cooked through, about 10 minutes.
3. Season with salt and black pepper.
4. Transfer the mixture to a blender, add heavy cream, and blend 'til smooth.
5. Chill before serving.

Per serving: Calories: 250kcal; Fat: 20g; Carbs: 2g; Protein: 12g

80. Beef Tallow Fat Bombs

Difficulty level: ★★★☆☆
Preparation time: 10 minutes
Cooking time: 5 minutes
Servings: 4
Ingredients:

- 1/2 cup beef tallow
- 1/4 cup cocoa powder
- 2 tbsp erythritol or sweetener of choice (optional)

Directions:

1. Melt the beef tallow in a small saucepan over low heat.
2. Stir in your cocoa powder and sweetener if using, 'til well combined.
3. Place mixture into silicone molds or a lined tray.
4. Refrigerate 'til solid.
5. Pop out of molds then store in the refrigerator.

Per serving: Calories: 150kcal; Fat: 15g; Carbs: 0g; Protein: 1g

101 Days Meal Plan

Day	Breakfast	Lunch	Snack	Dinner
1	Ham and Cheese Omelet	Pan-Seared Ribeye with Garlic Butter	Smoked Salmon Slices	Seared Scallops with Butter
2	Pork Belly Breakfast Bites	Pork Loin Cutlets	Prosciutto-Wrapped Mozzarella	Beef Kebabs with Simple Seasoning
3	Beef Liver and Egg Scramble	Meatballs in Bone Broth	Beef Tallow Fat Bombs	Lamb Burgers with Cheese
4	Chicken and Egg Scramble	Chicken Drumsticks with Ghee	Chicken Sausage Bites	Beef Strip Loin
5	Sausage and Cheese Frittata	Beef and Cheese Roll-Ups	Sliced Beef Jerky Chips	Butter-Basted Shrimp
6	Carnivore Breakfast Sausages	Beef Ribs with Simple Seasoning	Crispy Chicken Skins	Pan-Seared Salmon Steaks
7	Scrambled Eggs with Bacon	Shrimp Skewers with Herb Butter	Pork Rind Nachos	Ribeye Steak with Garlic Butter
8	Pork Chops and Eggs	Quick Grilled Lamb Chops	Chicken Liver Mousse	Herb-Crusted Lamb Chops

9	Lamb Chop Breakfast Plate	Grilled Chicken Breast with Butter	Shrimp Cocktail	Oven-Roasted Turkey Legs
10	Cheese and Egg Muffins	Carnivore Tuna Salad	Carnivore Cheese Board	Pork Shoulder Steaks
11	Crispy Bacon and Fried Eggs	Crispy Pork Rind Crusted Chicken	Sliced Salami	Sautéed Chicken Hearts
12	Steak and Egg Skillet	Carnivore Baked Meatloaf	Bacon Chips	Pork Tenderloin Medallions
13	Cheese-Stuffed Egg Bites	Beef Burger Patties with Cheese	Beef Jerky	Pork Spare Ribs
14	Ground Beef and Cheese Scramble	Simple Grilled Pork Tenderloin	Egg Salad	Pork Ribeye Chops
15	Beef Sausage Patties	Salmon Filets with Lemon Butter	Meat Sticks	Baked Chicken Wings
16	Egg and Beef Breakfast Bowl	Pan-Fried Tilapia with Butter	Beef Tallow Fat Bombs	Grilled Sirloin Steak

17	Carnivore Pancakes	Sliced Roast Beef with Mustard	Mini Meatballs	Beef Tenderloin Tips
18	Salmon and Cream Cheese Roll-Ups	Chicken Thighs with Skin-On	Liver Pate Bites	Pan-Fried Cod Fillets
19	Meat and Egg Breakfast Burrito	Bacon-Wrapped Chicken Breast	Ham Roll-Ups	Seared Ahi Tuna
20	Ribeye Steak and Eggs	Grilled Flank Steak	Pork Cracklings	Butter-Basted Shrimp
21	Pork Belly Breakfast Bites	Shrimp Skewers with Herb Butter	Smoked Salmon Slices	Lamb Burgers with Cheese
22	Beef Liver and Egg Scramble	Quick Grilled Lamb Chops	Prosciutto-Wrapped Mozzarella	Beef Strip Loin
23	Chicken and Egg Scramble	Grilled Chicken Breast with Butter	Carnivore Cheese Board	Baked Meat and Cheese Casserole

24	Scrambled Eggs with Bacon	Pan-Seared Ribeye with Garlic Butter	Crispy Chicken Skins	Pan-Seared Salmon Steaks
25	Pork Chops and Eggs	Pork Loin Cutlets	Pork Rind Nachos	Pork Shoulder Steaks
26	Lamb Chop Breakfast Plate	Carnivore Baked Meatloaf	Chicken Liver Mousse	Sautéed Chicken Hearts
27	Ground Beef and Cheese Scramble	Beef Burger Patties with Cheese	Shrimp Cocktail	Pork Tenderloin Medallions
28	Beef Sausage Patties	Simple Grilled Pork Tenderloin	Meat Sticks	Baked Chicken Wings
29	Egg and Beef Breakfast Bowl	Salmon Filets with Lemon Butter	Beef Tallow Fat Bombs	Grilled Sirloin Steak
30	Carnivore Pancakes	Bacon-Wrapped Chicken Breast	Mini Meatballs	Beef Tenderloin Tips

31	Ham and Cheese Omelet	Sliced Roast Beef with Mustard	Smoked Salmon Slices	Seared Scallops with Butter
32	Pork Belly Breakfast Bites	Chicken Thighs with Skin-On	Prosciutto-Wrapped Mozzarella	Beef Kebabs with Simple Seasoning
33	Beef Liver and Egg Scramble	Meatballs in Bone Broth	Beef Jerky	Lamb Burgers with Cheese
34	Chicken and Egg Scramble	Chicken Drumsticks with Ghee	Chicken Sausage Bites	Beef Strip Loin
35	Sausage and Cheese Frittata	Beef and Cheese Roll-Ups	Sliced Beef Jerky Chips	Baked Meat and Cheese Casserole
36	Carnivore Breakfast Sausages	Beef Ribs with Simple Seasoning	Crispy Chicken Skins	Pan-Seared Salmon Steaks
37	Scrambled Eggs with Bacon	Shrimp Skewers with Herb Butter	Pork Rind Nachos	Ribeye Steak with Garlic Butter
38	Pork Chops and Eggs	Quick Grilled Lamb Chops	Chicken Liver Mousse	Herb-Crusted Lamb Chops

39	Lamb Chop Breakfast Plate	Grilled Chicken Breast with Butter	Shrimp Cocktail	Oven-Roasted Turkey Legs
40	Cheese and Egg Muffins	Carnivore Tuna Salad	Carnivore Cheese Board	Pork Shoulder Steaks
41	Crispy Bacon and Fried Eggs	Crispy Pork Rind Crusted Chicken	Sliced Salami	Sautéed Chicken Hearts
42	Steak and Egg Skillet	Carnivore Baked Meatloaf	Bacon Chips	Pork Tenderloin Medallions
43	Cheese-Stuffed Egg Bites	Beef Burger Patties with Cheese	Beef Jerky	Pork Spare Ribs
44	Ground Beef and Cheese Scramble	Simple Grilled Pork Tenderloin	Egg Salad	Pork Ribeye Chops
45	Beef Sausage Patties	Salmon Filets with Lemon Butter	Meat Sticks	Baked Chicken Wings
46	Egg and Beef Breakfast Bowl	Pan-Fried Tilapia with Butter	Beef Tallow Fat Bombs	Grilled Sirloin Steak

47	Carnivore Pancakes	Pan-Seared Ribeye with Garlic Butter	Mini Meatballs	Beef Tenderloin Tips
48	Salmon and Cream Cheese Roll-Ups	Chicken Thighs with Skin-On	Liver Pate Bites	Pan-Fried Cod Fillets
49	Meat and Egg Breakfast Burrito	Bacon-Wrapped Chicken Breast	Ham Roll-Ups	Seared Ahi Tuna
50	Ribeye Steak and Eggs	Grilled Flank Steak	Pork Cracklings	Butter-Basted Shrimp
51	Pork Belly Breakfast Bites	Shrimp Skewers with Herb Butter	Smoked Salmon Slices	Lamb Burgers with Cheese
52	Beef Liver and Egg Scramble	Quick Grilled Lamb Chops	Prosciutto-Wrapped Mozzarella	Beef Kebabs with Simple Seasoning
53	Chicken and Egg Scramble	Grilled Chicken Breast with Butter	Carnivore Cheese Board	Baked Meat and Cheese Casserole
54	Scrambled Eggs with Bacon	Sliced Roast Beef with Mustard	Crispy Chicken Skins	Pan-Seared Salmon Steaks

55	Pork Chops and Eggs	Pork Loin Cutlets	Pork Rind Nachos	Pork Shoulder Steaks
56	Lamb Chop Breakfast Plate	Carnivore Baked Meatloaf	Chicken Liver Mousse	Sautéed Chicken Hearts
57	Ground Beef and Cheese Scramble	Beef Burger Patties with Cheese	Shrimp Cocktail	Pork Tenderloin Medallions
58	Beef Sausage Patties	Simple Grilled Pork Tenderloin	Meat Sticks	Baked Chicken Wings
59	Egg and Beef Breakfast Bowl	Salmon Filets with Lemon Butter	Beef Tallow Fat Bombs	Grilled Sirloin Steak
60	Carnivore Pancakes	Bacon-Wrapped Chicken Breast	Mini Meatballs	Beef Tenderloin Tips
61	Pork Belly Breakfast Bites	Pan-Seared Ribeye with Garlic Butter	Smoked Salmon Slices	Lamb Burgers with Cheese
62	Beef Liver and Egg Scramble	Chicken Thighs with Skin-On	Prosciutto-Wrapped Mozzarella	Beef Strip Loin

63	Chicken and Egg Scramble	Meatballs in Bone Broth	Beef Jerky	Baked Meat and Cheese Casserole
64	Sausage and Cheese Frittata	Chicken Drumsticks with Ghee	Chicken Sausage Bites	Pan-Fried Cod Fillets
65	Carnivore Breakfast Sausages	Beef and Cheese Roll-Ups	Sliced Beef Jerky Chips	Ribeye Steak with Garlic Butter
66	Scrambled Eggs with Bacon	Beef Ribs with Simple Seasoning	Crispy Chicken Skins	Herb-Crusted Lamb Chops
67	Pork Chops and Eggs	Shrimp Skewers with Herb Butter	Pork Rind Nachos	Oven-Roasted Turkey Legs
68	Ham and Cheese Omelet	Quick Grilled Lamb Chops	Chicken Liver Mousse	Pork Shoulder Steaks
69	Cheese and Egg Muffins	Grilled Chicken Breast with Butter	Shrimp Cocktail	Sautéed Chicken Hearts
70	Crispy Bacon and Fried Eggs	Carnivore Tuna Salad	Carnivore Cheese Board	Pork Tenderloin Medallions

71	Steak and Egg Skillet	Crispy Pork Rind Crusted Chicken	Sliced Salami	Pork Spare Ribs
72	Cheese-Stuffed Egg Bites	Carnivore Baked Meatloaf	Bacon Chips	Pork Ribeye Chops
73	Ground Beef and Cheese Scramble	Beef Burger Patties with Cheese	Beef Jerky	Baked Chicken Wings
74	Beef Sausage Patties	Simple Grilled Pork Tenderloin	Egg Salad	Grilled Sirloin Steak
75	Egg and Beef Breakfast Bowl	Salmon Filets with Lemon Butter	Meat Sticks	Beef Tenderloin Tips
76	Carnivore Pancakes	Pan-Fried Tilapia with Butter	Beef Tallow Fat Bombs	Pan-Seared Salmon Steaks
77	Salmon and Cream Cheese Roll-Ups	Sliced Roast Beef with Mustard	Mini Meatballs	Seared Ahi Tuna
78	Meat and Egg Breakfast Burrito	Chicken Thighs with Skin-On	Liver Pate Bites	Butter-Basted Shrimp

79	Ribeye Steak and Eggs	Bacon-Wrapped Chicken Breast	Ham Roll-Ups	Lamb Burgers with Cheese
80	Pork Belly Breakfast Bites	Grilled Flank Steak	Pork Cracklings	Beef Strip Loin
81	Beef Liver and Egg Scramble	Shrimp Skewers with Herb Butter	Smoked Salmon Slices	Baked Meat and Cheese Casserole
82	Chicken and Egg Scramble	Quick Grilled Lamb Chops	Prosciutto-Wrapped Mozzarella	Pan-Fried Cod Fillets
83	Scrambled Eggs with Bacon	Grilled Chicken Breast with Butter	Carnivore Cheese Board	Pork Shoulder Steaks
84	Pork Chops and Eggs	Pan-Seared Ribeye with Garlic Butter	Crispy Chicken Skins	Sautéed Chicken Hearts
85	Lamb Chop Breakfast Plate	Pork Loin Cutlets	Pork Rind Nachos	Pork Tenderloin Medallions
86	Ground Beef and Cheese Scramble	Carnivore Baked Meatloaf	Chicken Liver Mousse	Baked Chicken Wings

87	Beef Sausage Patties	Beef Burger Patties with Cheese	Shrimp Cocktail	Grilled Sirloin Steak
88	Egg and Beef Breakfast Bowl	Simple Grilled Pork Tenderloin	Meat Sticks	Beef Tenderloin Tips
89	Carnivore Pancakes	Salmon Filets with Lemon Butter	Beef Tallow Fat Bombs	Seared Scallops with Butter
90	Ham and Cheese Omelet	Bacon-Wrapped Chicken Breast	Mini Meatballs	Beef Kebabs with Simple Seasoning
91	Beef Liver and Egg Scramble	Sliced Roast Beef with Mustard	Carnivore Cheese Board	Pork Ribeye Chops
92	Chicken and Egg Scramble	Pork Loin Cutlets	Chicken Sausage Bites	Seared Ahi Tuna
93	Sausage and Cheese Frittata	Meatballs in Bone Broth	Sliced Beef Jerky Chips	Lamb Burgers with Cheese
94	Carnivore Breakfast Sausages	Chicken Drumsticks with Ghee	Crispy Chicken Skins	Beef Strip Loin

95	Scrambled Eggs with Bacon	Beef and Cheese Roll-Ups	Pork Rind Nachos	Baked Meat and Cheese Casserole
96	Pork Chops and Eggs	Beef Ribs with Simple Seasoning	Chicken Liver Mousse	Pan-Seared Salmon Steaks
97	Lamb Chop Breakfast Plate	Shrimp Skewers with Herb Butter	Shrimp Cocktail	Ribeye Steak with Garlic Butter
98	Cheese and Egg Muffins	Quick Grilled Lamb Chops	Beef Tallow Fat Bombs	Herb-Crusted Lamb Chops
99	Crispy Bacon and Fried Eggs	Grilled Chicken Breast with Butter	Sliced Salami	Oven-Roasted Turkey Legs
100	Steak and Egg Skillet	Carnivore Tuna Salad	Bacon Chips	Pork Shoulder Steaks
101	Cheese-Stuffed Egg Bites	Crispy Pork Rind Crusted Chicken	Beef Jerky	Sautéed Chicken Hearts

Shopping List

Meat & Seafood

- Bacon
- Beef liver
- Beef ribs
- Beef sirloin
- Beef strip loins
- Beef tenderloin
- Chicken breasts
- Chicken drumsticks
- Chicken hearts
- Chicken liver
- Chicken sausages
- Chicken thighs
- Cod fillets
- Flank steak
- Ground beef
- Ground lamb
- Ground pork
- Ham
- Lamb chops
- Pork belly
- Pork chops
- Pork loin cutlets
- Pork ribeye chops
- Pork shoulder steaks
- Pork spare ribs
- Pork tenderloin
- Ribeye steaks
- Roast beef
- Salmon filets
- Salmon steaks
- Sausage
- Scallops
- Shrimp
- Sirloin steaks
- Smoked salmon
- Tilapia filets
- Tuna steak
- Turkey legs
- Ahi tuna steaks
- Pepperoni slices
- Prosciutto slices
- Salami slices
- Chicken wings

Dairy & Cheese

- Aged Parmesan
- Cheddar cheese
- Cream cheese
- Gouda cheese
- Heavy cream
- Mozzarella cheese
- Shredded cheddar cheese
- Shredded mozzarella cheese
- Sour cream

Pantry Staples

- Bone broth
- Dijon or yellow mustard
- Garlic powder
- Onion powder
- Olive oil
- Paprika
- Pork rinds
- Soy sauce
- Worcestershire sauce
- Beef tallow
- Cocoa powder
- Erythritol (optional)

Spices & Herbs

- Black pepper
- Dried oregano (optional)
- Dried parsley
- Dried rosemary
- Dried thyme
- Fresh chives (optional)
- Fresh dill (optional)
- Garlic cloves
- Salt
- Sesame seeds (optional)
- Smoked paprika (optional)

Fats & Oils

- Butter
- Ghee
- Unsalted butter
- Mayonnaise

Eggs

- Eggs

Vegetables & Other

- Capers (optional)
- Jalapeños (optional)
- Lemon juice (optional)
- Mustard (optional)
- Onions

Other Protein Snacks

- Beef jerky

Conclusion

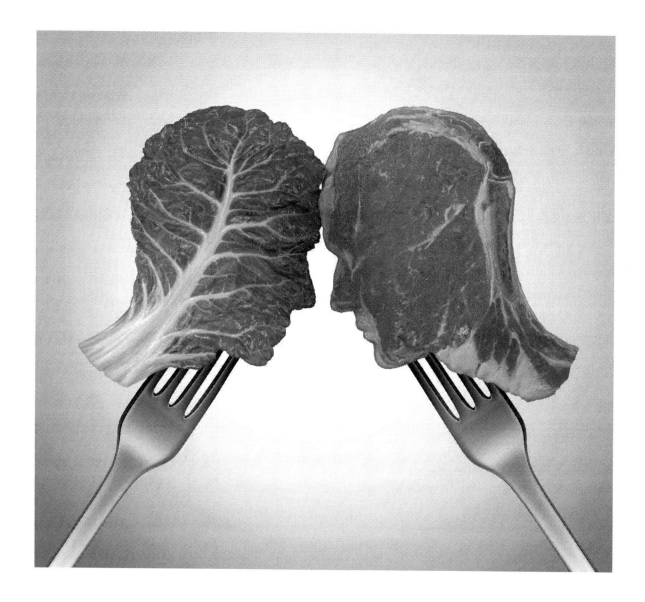

The Carnivore Diet is a unique and powerful approach that focuses exclusively on animal-based foods, offering a radical departure from traditional dietary guidelines. Rooted in the consumption of meats, fish, eggs, and animal fats, the diet simplifies nutrition by eliminating all plant-based foods, sugars, and processed carbohydrates. This approach aims to reset the body's metabolism, reduce inflammation, and improve overall health by leveraging the high nutrient density of animal products.

For many, the Carnivore Diet has proven effective for weight loss, improved mental clarity, increased energy, and better management of chronic conditions like autoimmune diseases and digestive disorders. Its high protein and fat content supports muscle growth and satiety, making it easier to adhere to for those who struggle with constant hunger on other diets. Additionally, the diet's simplicity—focusing on whole, unprocessed foods—eliminates the guesswork around meal planning and nutrient intake.

However, like any dietary plan, it is not without its challenges. Adapting to the lack of variety, potential nutrient deficiencies if not carefully managed, and social restrictions can be hurdles for some individuals. It's crucial for those considering the Carnivore Diet to educate themselves, consult with healthcare professionals, and listen to their bodies.

Ultimately, the Carnivore Diet offers a compelling option for those seeking a straightforward, whole-food approach to nutrition that prioritizes animal-based foods. Whether used as a short-term reset or a long-term lifestyle, it has the potential to significantly impact health and well-being for those who thrive on this ancestral way of eating.

Index

Salmon Filets with Lemon Butter; 44
Sausage and Cheese Frittata; 38
Sautéed Chicken Hearts; 66
Scrambled Eggs with Bacon; 27
Seared Ahi Tuna; 65
Seared Scallops with Butter; 57
Shrimp Cocktail; 75

Shrimp Skewers with Herb Butter; 47
Simple Grilled Pork Tenderloin; 48
Sliced Beef Jerky Chips; 73
Sliced Roast Beef with Mustard; 46
Sliced Salami; 78
Smoked Salmon Slices; 72
Steak and Egg Skillet; 27

Made in United States
Orlando, FL
05 December 2024

55015721R00054